Awaken

VERB: awak· en | ə-ˈwā-kən

1. Rouse from sleep; cause to stop sleeping.
2. Regain consciousness.
3. Become aware of; come to a realization of.
4. Make or become active again.

Jurgen Matthesius

Published by Awaken Press, San Diego, California, USA AwakenChurch.com Copyright © 2020 Jurgen Matthesius Printed in the United States of America Unless otherwise stated, all Scripture quotations are taken from the New King James Version®. Copyright © 1982 by Thomas Nelson. Used by permission. All rights reserved. Scripture quotations marked AMP are taken from the Amplified® Bible, Copyright © 1954, 1958, 1962, 1964, 1965, 1987 by The Lockman Foundation. Used by permission. (wvvw.Lockrnan.org) Scripture quotations marked CEV are from the Contemporary English Version Copyright © 1991, 1992, 1995 by American Bible Society, Used by Permission. Scripture quotations marked ESV are from the ESV® Bible (The Holy Bible, English Standard Version®), copyright © 2001 by Crossway, a publishing ministry of Good News Publishers. Used by permission. All rights reserved. Scripture quotations marked KJV are taken from the King James Version. Scripture quotations from THE MESSAGE. Copyright © by Eugene H. Peterson 1993, 1994, 1995, 1996, 2000, 2001, 2002. Used by permission of Tyndale House Publishers, Inc. Scripture quotations marked NASB are taken from the New American Standard Bible®, Copyright © 1960, 1962, 1963, 1968, 1971, 1972, 1973, 1975, 1977, 1995 by The Lockman Foundation Used by permission. Scripture quotations marked NIV are taken from the Holy Bible, New International Version®, NIV®. Copyright © 1973, 1978, 1984, 2011 by Biblica, Inc.Tm Used by permission of Zondervan. All rights reserved worldwide. www.zondervan.com The "NIV" and "New International Version" are trademarks registered in the United States Patent and Trademark Office by Biblica, Inc. TM Scripture quotations marked NLT are taken from the Holy Bible, New Living Translation, copyright ©1996, 2004, 2007, 2013 by Tyndale House Foundation. Used by permission of Tyndale House Publishers, Inc., Carol Stream, Illinois 60188. All rights reserved. Note: Some quotations from the New Living Translation are taken from earlier editions. Scripture quotations marked TEV are taken from the Good News Translation in Today's English Version- Second Edition Copyright © 1992 by American Bible Society. Used by permission. Any italicization or words in brackets added to scripture quotations are the author's additions for emphasis or clarity. All rights reserved. No part of this publication may be reproduced, distributed, or transmitted in any form or by any means, including photocopying, recording, or other electronic or mechanical methods, without the prior written permission of the publisher, except in the case of brief quotations embodied in critical reviews and certain other noncommercial uses permitted by copyright law.

Dedication

Firstly, I would like to dedicate this book to my beautiful bride, my love, my helper, my companion, my princess Leanne Matthesius, without whom none of the great things in my life would have been accomplished. Her wisdom, support, encouragement, and resolve to challenge me where I need it has been an immeasurable source of strength and blessing to my life. I would not be who or what I am without the magnificent 'helper' the Lord blessed me to do life with. I love you!

I'd also like to thank my amazing family and team. They say that "Life moves at the speed of relationships," and we are able to move at an extraordinary pace because of the great relationships in our world. We are so rich and blessed. Our kids and our team are a continual source of joy and delight, making the journey an ever-unfolding adventure filled with fun, excitement, and anticipation of even greater things!

Awaken to life beyond what you've imagined

Awaken to a higher purpose and reality

Awaken to the place beyond your dreams

Awaken to all that God has for you

Contents

Introduction: *The Story of* **Awaken** 7

Chapter 1: **Awaken** *To A New Reality* 19

Chapter 2: **Awaken** *To A New Expression* 29

Chapter 3: **Awaken** *To A New Experience* 37

Chapter 4: **Awaken** *To The Culture Clash* 47

Chapter 5: **Awaken** *To A New Mission* 57

Chapter 6: **Awaken** *Divine Flows* 69

Chapter 7: **Awaken** *Divine Devotion* 85

Get To Know Pastor: **Jurgen & Leanne** 99

INTRODUCTION

The Story of
Awaken

SEVENS

It was January of 1986 when I was invited to a Christian surfers' event, hoping to do well and perhaps secure a sponsorship deal. I had no idea what was about to happen, and nothing could have prepared me for what I was about to experience. Placing fourth in the event ultimately did lead to a wetsuit sponsorship deal; however, what I received that weekend can only be described as my first AWAKEN experience. I was suddenly thrust into a world that I previously had no idea existed.

In 1990, I decided to leave my studies in mechanical engineering to attend Power Ministry School Bible College, which is known today as Hillsong College. After graduating at the end of 1991, my family and I moved to Manukau City, where I became a youth pastor at South City Christian Life Center. We would spend the next seven years there, falling in love with the nation of New Zealand, its culture, and its wonderful people (not to mention the All Blacks rugby team and Whittaker's chocolate). These seven learning years would AWAKEN us to the need for ministry in our cities, to the potency of a vibrant, life-giving church, and to the impact the gospel of Jesus Christ has on lives. We saw thousands of people's lives radically changed for eternity.

We also became aware of the value of having fun while undertaking the burden of seeing a city and a nation changed. We learned to value the treasure of friendship, and many of these people have become lifelong friends. We learned how to and how NOT to treat people. We experienced firsthand the need for leadership in both the church and in the community. We learned that if we are not leading ourselves healthily, we have no authority to lead others. Because of the strong Maori Indigenous culture, we also learned a lot about the power of spiritual influences on communities, mindsets, and our physical lives. Because of that, we were AWOKEN to the power of the gospel and how it can break the demonic strongholds over people's lives to set them free from destructive paths, patterns, paradigms, and powers!

Leanne and I learned the importance of our relationship with one another. We spent so many years fighting with each other before we AWOKE to the reality that we needed to be fighting FOR one another instead. It was also here that God blessed us, and we became a family. Our first two sons, Jordan and Ashley, would be born here -- magnificent gifts from God for whom I am eternally grateful to be their dad. We also had an AWAKENing to the importance of rest and observing the Sabbath. But perhaps the greatest AWAKEN experience would be the power we discovered when the gift of FAITH was released through PRAYER (this concept would ultimately shape the genesis for my book PUSH).

In 1998, we were called back to Australia through the same prophet who, seven years earlier, had told us God had called us to New Zealand. We were told that our days in New Zealand were numbered and that "God was calling us back to Australia" – not to where we had come from, but instead to a church that moves in the power of the Holy Spirit. "Enough of this preaching gift," the prophet said. "You are called to have a power ministry!" As I lay there slain in the Spirit, the only church that came to mind that even remotely resembled that word was Pastor Phil Pringle's church. I thought to myself, "He wouldn't know me from Adam!" However, through a series of fortuitous events, we became the youth pastors at Christian City Church in Oxford Falls, Sydney, under the extraordinary leadership of pastors Phil and Chris Pringle.

This would be another seven-year tenor that would AWAKEN us to concepts like "the Big Hug" (how to do life through a team as opposed to achieving goals through a staff) and "the POWER of the Holy Spirit" (moving from seeing the Holy Spirit as an "optional extra" to seeing Him and His limitless wisdom as your greatest ally in building the church and seeing lives set free). We learned how to move and flow in the gifts and presence of the Holy Spirit. It was a life-changing season. The stories we would read in the gospel and the book of ACTS were happening each and every week in and through our lives. The entire Bible came ALIVE.

We also had an AWAKEN experience to God's resourcing for His kingdom, namely the power of money. We would witness firsthand the integrity our senior pastors and team operated in as they handled and released millions of dollars to advance the kingdom in our community, city, nation, and around the world through the acquisitions of property, building schools, including a world-class creative arts and leadership college, to funding missions work in third-world nations and many other amazing ventures. It was here we learned how to overcome the power of money – what the Bible calls "the spirit of mammon"—through generosity, sacrificial giving, and faithful tithing. It was here that I was AWOKEN to the truth that if you have power over money, it will be attracted to you; however, if money has power over you, it will be repelled from you.

Giving is the EXERCISE of power over money. If you have something you cannot give, then you don't have it; it has you!

We had such a radical mindset change that by our seventh year, we were giving away more than we had earned in our first year. This would be one of the greatest AWAKENing seasons of our lives and one that made us so grateful for the spiritual parents God had sent us in Pastors Phil and Christine Pringle. In fact, so indelibly had our lives been impacted and shaped here that my heart pledged to serve Phil and Chris for the rest of our lives. In all sincerity, I wanted to be buried in the grounds at Oxford Falls. We were completely different people on every level: the health of our walk with God, our relationship with each other, and our finances. We had no desire to leave – ever. However, as God usually does, this would be the time when he would kick the "baby eagle" out of the nest and have it learn to fly on its own. In 2005, Pastor Phil had me come into his office and asked what I felt for the next chapter of our lives. He then said he felt there was "a church inside of us" and wanted us to pray about starting one. I said, "Okay, how about the Gold Coast of Australia?" (I was thinking of beaches, warm water, surfing, housing half the price of Sydney and a way to stay in Australia close to family). Pastor Phil said, "No, I want you to pray about San Diego. I've always wanted a church in San Diego." I thought, "San Diego? That's not even in Australia!?"

But in July of 2005, we found ourselves moving to San Diego to start what was then Christian City Church San Diego. My wife Leanne and my three sons Jordan, Ashley, and Tommy were along on the journey, and it was certainly not easy, especially for our eldest son, who was ten years old, leaving all of his friends behind and moving countries for the second time. It bore a heavy toll on him, and I can remember him trying not to let me see his pain while sitting across from me on the plane. It was our greatest adventure and, at the same time, the largest risk we had ever undertaken. To float the vision, we had put $100,000 on our mortgage in Australia and launched out believing that such obedience might be met with the same level of benevolence from the God we were serving. This would AWAKEN us to the reality that the same God who watched over us as we served Him in New Zealand and who brought us to the Northern beaches would be the same God who would show us His mighty power and provision in America.

BEGINNINGS, BELIEFS, and BATTLES

We started with 21 people at a prayer meeting on a Wednesday evening at our home in Scripps Ranch, a subdivision in San Diego. As discussions around vision, mission, and culture began to flow, we received warnings (well-intended warnings) that we should avoid becoming a spirit-filled church. Moving in the Spirit was looked down upon. It was considered "weird" and definitely not something we wanted to be associated with – not if we wanted to build a big church or reach unchurched people. We were told that Southern California was a "Calvinist theology stronghold" and that there were no spirit-filled churches over 300 people. The advice was that if we wanted to build a "city-influencing church," we needed to stay far away from the gifts of the spirit. In fact, it would be better if we could avoid the Holy Spirit altogether, as He is considered to be rather "reckless" when it comes to church and people.

These taboo topics, we were told, would minimize church growth and drive people away. San Diego folks were not interested in having an encounter with God but preferred to turn up and experience "church as usual." Cater to this, we were told, and we could maintain a good life as a pastor. The second piece of advice we received is that we should never speak about money. We were told San Diego was a Materialistic state. The last thing you want to do is touch people's treasure. If you want to keep them coming on a Sunday, do not speak about money. We were told speaking about money would offend people, thus driving them away from our church.

The third taboo we were told to avoid was to never engage, appoint, or empower women to preach, teach, or lead from the platform. No, no, no, no! We were told that San Diego's theology had been permanently shaped by a theology that forbade this practice. We received quite the admonition that the apostle Paul had made it clear: "Women were to sit silently in church, not to engage in any significant or meaningful way. They were to show their support by cooking great meals at home, watching the children, perhaps even playing the piano or arranging the flowers. Women were to be seen and not heard." *They were more like God's adornments, smiling but silent flowers, reminding us all that even God makes mistakes from time to time.* After all, it wasn't Adam who sinned; it was Eve. So, according to their theology, if it wasn't for Eve (the woman), we wouldn't be in this mess in the first place, and God (who apparently has a hard time with forgiveness, redemption, and restoration) now prefers that we keep women far away from any kind of influence or authority.

As crazy as all these taboos sound, they were highly influential for me. They helped me crystallize and clarify what kind of church we were going to build. We knew God wasn't sending us to San Diego to give San Diegans what they already had. *We also knew that to have authority over the culture of a city, we couldn't become infected by the culture of that city.* The city has what it has because of its culture.

The kingdom of God operates and flows through a certain culture. Our job is to overthrow anything in the culture influenced by the demonic and replace it with Kingdom Culture, inspired by the Holy Spirit, thereby SEEING God's power move mightily in our city. Besides, we knew we had given up too much and sacrificed too greatly to give San Diego more of what it already had. God knew what he wanted to plant and grow in San Diego, and that's why He was sending us. *We refused to allow the broken church culture in San Diego to dictate the tune, melody, and lyrics of the song our church would bring to shift this city towards Christ.*

We believe that the church, like every healthy home, should have a mother's voice and a father's voice. Throughout the Bible, we see women prophesying, leading, ministering, and proclaiming. These examples contradict the message of some modern doctrinal beliefs that have built an almost cult-like following around Paul's admonition in 1 Corinthians 14:34, that women should "keep silence" in church. Scottish theologian William Barclay (1907- 1978) explains that the book of Corinthians was written to a specific church to address specific problems that the church was facing. In this case, the problem being addressed is related to order and orderliness. During the time of Paul's writing, the women of Corinth were not in order. They were being disruptive to the public service. They were unruly, and, as Barclay notes, Paul did not want any immodesty or slight of character to be a blight on the early church.

Additionally, women of that era would not have had the education necessary to teach because tutelage under a rabbi would have been a privilege only available to men. Paul told the women to ask their husbands if they had questions; they were encouraged to seek out knowledge, but in the absence of formal teaching opportunities, this was the "cultural order" of the day. Erring on the side of caution, Barclay says, Paul told women not to speak.

However, Paul's words of correction to the church in Corinth do not mean that all women should be excluded from platform ministry. We see exemplary church leadership in women like Miriam, Deborah, Esther, Huldah, Athiliah, Anna, and Priscilla, whom Paul calls a "fellow worker" in Christ Jesus (Romans 16:3). Phoebe was a deaconess in the early church and the books of Luke, Acts, and Judges all mention "certain women" who positively impacted the house of God. Jesus himself shattered the shame of first-century women by talking with them openly and including them in his ministry.

In fact, there is a scholarly consensus that the early church actually owes its growth to women, who spread the gospel in the modern equivalent of water cooler conversations — women at the well and the river sharing the good news of Jesus and impacting households, emperors, and empires. Women were the local missionaries and mouthpieces of the early church. Throughout history, God has been in the business of empowering both men and women and providing them with ministry opportunities.

God created women to be by man's side as a helper. One of the first things God said after creating man was that it was not good that man should be alone; in other words, God was saying not only did Eve complete Adam, but she was created for him to fulfill his mission. He cannot do it without her. This is why we love to empower our women to rise up and step into their divine calling: to minister, to preach, to lead, and to disciple.

At Awaken, you will see us move in the gifts and release the power of the Holy Spirit. We are not so presumptuous that we believe we can build the church in the power of humanistic strategy and education. We do not believe that the art of man can sustain what the armor of God has established. We believe the Holy Spirit is sent to empower us, lead and guide, equip and resource, and give wisdom and divine understanding on how we can navigate the complexities of our current culture and community. Because of this, we regularly see miracles, signs, and wonders.

At Awaken Church, you will have an encounter with the third person of the Trinity, the Holy Spirit, and you will receive power. You will speak in new tongues. You will experience the supernatural, and you will experience the gifts of the spirit flowing through your life and operating in you to bring breakthrough to other people. *At Awaken Church, you will experience the intersection between two dimensions, the heavenly realm and the earthly realm combining in your life as God begins to mold you into a divine instrument of his mercy, power, loving kindness, and grace in the earth.*

At Awaken Church, we have no hesitations speaking about money. We believe God wants to prosper you. The Bible teaches biblical principles for an abundant life and shows you how to increase and multiply. God created you to be the head, not the tail, to be above only and not beneath. You were created not only to receive the blessing of God upon your life but also to bestow it on those around you. He is the God of more than enough.

Luke 6:37 says that as you give, it will be given to you. "A good measure, pressed down, shaken together and running over will be poured into your lap." We believe the tithe opens the windows of heaven and pours out such a blessing that, as Malachi 3:10 says, "there will not be room enough to receive it." We believe the world of the generous gets larger and larger while the world of the stingy gets smaller and smaller. As Proverbs 11:24-25 says, "One person gives freely, yet gains even more; another withholds unduly, but comes to poverty. A generous person will prosper."

At Awaken Church, you'll find yourself flourishing like you've never flourished before. You're going to find that as you walk in the blessing of God, you will become a blessing to others, destroying the curse that is choking out people's hope and future. As you apply these principles to your life, you will begin living your best life now. You're going to find yourself flourishing. You're going to find yourself increasing beyond your wildest dreams and experiencing life the way God intended it. At Awaken Church, we don't believe you have to die to experience heaven; we believe the moment you are born again, heaven's reality begins to flow toward you, and as you line up your life with the principles in the scriptures and the principles written in the word of God, you come into a divine alignment. Heaven's reality, heaven's joy, and heaven's peace begin to flow so abundantly that when people look at your life, they'll ask, "Hey, dude, what are you on?"

Let's jump into chapter one.

CHAPTER ONE

Awaken To A New Reality

SALVATION, REDEMPTION, TRANSFORMATION.

"And Jacob went out from Beer-sheba, and went toward Haran. And he lighted upon a certain place, and tarried there all night, because the sun was set; and he took one of the stones of the place, and put it under his head, and lay down in that place to sleep. And he dreamed; and behold, a ladder set up on the earth, and the top of it reached to heaven; and behold, the angels of God ascending and descending on it. And, behold, Jehovah stood above it, and said, I am Jehovah, the God of Abraham thy father, and the God of Isaac: the land whereon thou liest, to thee will I give it, and to thy seed; and thy seed shall be as the dust of the earth, and thou shalt spread abroad to the west, and to the east, and to the north, and to the south: and in thee and in thy seed shall all the families of the earth be blessed. And, behold, I am with thee, and will keep thee whithersoever thou goest, and will bring thee again into this

land; for I will not leave thee, until I have done that which I have spoken to thee of. And Jacob awaked out of his sleep, and he said, Surely Jehovah is in this place; and I knew it not. And he was afraid, and said, How dreadful is this place! this is none other than the house of God, and this is the gate of heaven." Genesis 28:10-17 ASV

It was January of 1986 when I was 18 years old, clueless about where I wanted to go in life. All I knew at that time was that I loved Surfing because it brought me joy and peace. The elation of paddling out into the waves was like being immersed in the very heart of nature itself. "Maybe I could do something in the surfing industry and be paid for it," I thought to myself. "It wouldn't even need to be much, as the exhilaration and freedom of that lifestyle would be payment and reward enough." I had written to a few surf companies I knew were sponsors of other guys in my city, and I sent them my contest results. One company, Piping Hot Wetsuits, wrote back and said they were interested, but I needed to place in or win a major competition. Sponsorship was the pathway toward the goal of being paid to do what I loved – surfing. Still, it also would provide a balm of healing and credibility to a young man suffering rejection while searching for significance.

A friend told me about the JESUS Pro-Am being held at one of my favorite beaches, Caves Beach on the south coast. It was run and organized by Christian surfers. I thought, *"Christians? Are they even allowed to surf?"* In my very limited experience (namely a brief observation of ISCF, Inter School Christian Fellowship), I thought Christianity was defined by the "fun" things I no longer do because of a commitment to a Jewish man who died by Crucifixion 2,000 years ago. I figured the competition would be like taking candy from a baby. The only Christians I knew were bland, boring, androgynous goody-two-shoes who seemed like androids void of any passion, personality, or ambition. Yes! This could be the opportunity I was waiting for. I began to picture myself on the podium lifting up the first-place trophy above my head while the bewildered "Christians" clapped feebly, unsure whether it was holy to celebrate human accomplishment and achievement.

To my surprise, the weekend was completely opposite of what I had envisioned. The surf, despite a bleak forecast, was double overhead, and the level of skill was as high as I had seen at any professional event. These guys were shredding. *"This was not going to be easy,"* I thought. *"Obviously, other people must have heard about this opportunity to steal from these goody-two-shoes Christians!"* Then I found out these bronzed bodied, bleached haired, shredders WERE Christians! I placed fourth, and the guy who placed first shared his story in his acceptance speech. I had no idea he was preaching and sharing his testimony. He had earned the win with a phenomenal backhand 360 on a 4-foot close out to score a 9.2 ride, so I figured I owed it to him to listen to whatever he was saying in his first-place acceptance speech. He shared about Jesus, and what he had done on the cross, and how he had been saved. I had NEVER heard anything like this before, and when he got everyone to bow their heads for prayer, I hesitatingly looked around to make sure I wasn't the only one getting sucked in by some weird cult.

The next thing I knew, it seemed like he was speaking DIRECTLY to me. He described my life perfectly with one sentence: empty, searching for meaning, using people and things to try and fill a void in my soul that never seemed to satisfy. He then asked for anyone who related to raise their hands if they wanted Christ to come into their heart, fill that void, and forgive them of their sins. I wasn't exactly sure what it all meant, but I was 100 percent sure I wanted what he was speaking about. So, I closed my eyes, raised my hand, and prayed the prayer. All I know is when I opened my eyes after the word *"amen,"* EVERYTHING changed.

Even though I was still in the same identical place I was in before I prayed, every tree, every branch, every leaf, every person, every blade of grass was the same... and yet, something had happened. The whole world was the same, yet the whole world was different. I had no idea I was now *"born again."* The only way I could describe it was that it was like my whole life had been a dream, and I had now awakened from that dream. From that moment, my life has never been the same again. I had AWOKEN to a new reality. God, whoever He was, had become REAL to me. My life felt complete, attached to some divine meaning for the first time. I didn't know what it all meant, but it was good – the best feeling I had ever had, and I was NOT going to let it go.

Can you imagine waking up and discovering that you're in a completely different dimension? Whether it's Alice in Wonderland or Neo after taking the red pill in The Matrix, many movies and stories prophetically describe the reality and possibility of awakening to the existence of another dimension. Imagine you went to sleep in one place but woke up in a completely different time zone, era, country, or reality. This is akin to what Jacob experienced at a place he called Bethel (meaning *house of God*).

In Genesis chapter 28, Jacob put his head on a rock that he used as a pillow to sleep. He had no idea that the ground he was lying on was a land that had been spoken over by the one true God. God had promised Abraham, Jacob's grandfather, that this land would one day be the land of his descendants. Jacob had heard those words, but only from his father Isaac, who retold them to Jacob and his brother Esau when they were young boys. But here in this dream, he was hearing it from God himself. He saw a ladder set up between earth and heaven with angels ascending and descending upon it. He had no idea that these two realms could be connected and that there was a divine fence and interplay between them.

Genesis 28 tells the story of Jacob sojourning to a foreign country. As he sleeps, he dreams, and in his dream, he sees a ladder set up between earth and heaven with angels ascending and descending upon this ladder. Above the ladder is the Lord. God speaks to him, reiterating the promises that he had spoken to Jacob's forefathers, that "this would be the land that Jacob and his descendants would inherit, and that Jacob would become a mighty nation," blessed of God. Jacob would be a source of blessing for the entire world. He would carry the legacy and the blessings that God promised to Abraham, the faithful man of God, Jacob's grandfather. Jacob proclaims this is none other than the house of God.

He cries aloud, "How awesome is this place? This is the gate of heaven!"

At Awaken Church, this is exactly what you're going to experience. The church is the gateway to an entirely different realm. It is the gateway to a new reality. In heaven, there is perfect peace and justice. Here on the earth, there's war, strife, conflict, corruption, distortion, and oppression. But now that you are in God's house, there is a gateway set up between these two realms that enables you, through faith, to experience God's peace, justice, and power. There exists in this gateway a ladder where the angels of God ascend and descend, carrying our prayers to the throne of God and bringing back answers, breakthroughs, healings, and miracles. At Awaken Church, we believe the church is an awesome and holy place. The local church is the house of God, the gate of heaven. We believe God's presence longs to come dwell with us as we worship each Sunday so we can experience His presence and power.

Jacob's entire life changed at this place. At Awaken Church, we believe the same will happen for you. As you come into this place, you will encounter the living God, the reality of His promises, and

His goodness toward you. You will begin to believe, see, envision, and dream of a greater future.

I love the word awaken. God awakened Jacob to a new reality. Prior to that moment, Jacob was completely unaware that there was a fourth dimension, a spiritual dimension, working for him on his behalf. He had no idea that this God was a covenant-working God who was faithful in keeping His promises. He had no idea this God was a God who had blessing in mind for his children. If you know anything about Jacob, you know he did not deserve this blessing. This is actually good news because neither do we. God does not give to us according to our behavior; instead, his motivation is His great love for us. Because of this love, He gave us His most precious possession, His only begotten son. John 3:16 says, *"For God so loved the world that He gave His only begotten son, that whosoever would believe in Him would not perish but have everlasting life."*

Adam was created and formed by God from the dust of the earth. Adam was an inanimate creature, fully formed both internally and externally. He had a heart, lungs, feet, hands, eyes, and ears. He had a cardiovascular system, a reproductive system, a digestive system, a respiratory system, an immune system, and a central nervous system, all lying dormant, waiting for activation. Then suddenly, simultaneously, the face of God came over the face of Adam, and God breathed into Adam the breath of life, and Adam became a living being.

At Awaken Church, we believe in creating an atmosphere where the great breath and Spirit of God can flow into you so that you can awaken to a new reality with God. The Bible calls this being "born again," but it goes far beyond the religious context and use of that word. It means the Spirit of God will cause you to come to life, awakening all the things in you that were placed there by God before you were born. You will find your gifts, your callings, your potential call awakening, and you will begin to dream in direct congruency with your gifts and your calling. You will begin to understand your purpose and divine destiny. There is nothing greater than discovering the "WHY" behind the "when" you were born.

At AWAKEN Church, we have seven distinct values:

1. BIG CHURCH, BIG PICTURE

We are one church in multiple campuses, not multiple campuses that make up one church. Between campuses there is friendly competition that builds up and strengthens connection. It's not divisive competition that ends up dividing teams and tearing down morale. We want people to get planted in a campus that helps them to stay planted in our church. We want to give them permission and a roadmap to change campuses but not to "campus hop."

2. DISCIPLESHIP AND DEVELOPMENT

Without discipleship, there is no development, and without development, there is no discipleship. Our Pathway of Discipleship is our unique, strategic roadmap for our members to walk out their journey in community. We expound on this pathway in our DNA classes.

3. KNOWN>LOVED>WANTED>NEEDED

As a church, we are not just friendly; we know how to be a friend. As members connect, they become known, and then they realize that they are loved. As they realize they are truly known and truly loved, they realize they are truly wanted in the church community. That feeling awakens purpose, and they see how their gifts are needed to build the church.

4. PRAY UNTIL SOMETHING HAPPENS

We are a faith church. We speak the word of God, and signs and wonders follow us. We pray from a place of authority and not from wishful thinking. Awaken Church awakens faith in its members and in this city.

5. HEALING, FRUITFULNESS, AND PROSPERITY

There are three "supernatural wells" that our church is known for that flow to bring people from sickness to healing, from barrenness to fruitfulness, and from poverty to prosperity.

6. CULTURE OF HONOR

We honor not just our earthly fathers and mothers but all those in leadership over our lives. We honor their position and sacrifice so that it goes well for us.

7. DEPENDENT UPON THE WATERS ABOVE

We are individually responsible for our connection with God. We turn up on a Sunday to soak as well as to serve, and we serve from the overflow of the quiet time that we create uniquely for ourselves. Ocean water is undrinkable, but the rains that fall from the heavens above give life to every living thing. In the same way, we drink from and feed upon that which is from above, the heavenly realm, so that we might influence the earthly realm beneath.

CHAPTER TWO

Awaken To A New Expression

THE HOLY SPIRIT

It was Jan. 2, 1989. The deafening metal sound of the band Stryper was playing *"To Hell With the Devil"* and *"Soldiers Under Command"* as we ascended Mount Ousley in the southern city town of Wollongong. I had never been so pumped and motivated to attend a prayer meeting in my life. I had heard about this prayer meeting, and it was powerful. It was positioned on a cliff top overlooking the entire city lights of the beautiful city of Wollongong, which lay silently dormant beneath. We were the prayer warriors; we were those who were going to do battle in the spiritual realm for the souls of the city beneath. We always began with worship, led by Pastor Chuck. It was after the third song describing the greatness of God that Pastor Chuck stopped playing his guitar, looked directly at me, and asked, "Have you been baptized with the Holy Spirit?" I responded, "I've been water baptized!" He said, "No, I'm talking about an infilling of the power of the Holy Spirit!" I told him I had not. He then asked everybody to lay hands on me, and before I knew it, I hit the ground, solid concrete, and as I lay there, I began to speak in languages I've never learned.

Up until that time, Bible reading was a chore. I would read the Bible dutifully every day because I knew that was what I needed to do to be a Christian; however, I found it dry and burdensome. But after receiving the Holy Spirit, I went home that night and read my Bible for the next three hours. It was like the words were swimming on the page. It was like I was sitting down with the author of the book who was showing me things in the subtext, in the pretext, hidden not from me but hidden for me. The Bible came alive – heck, the Christian faith came alive! Suddenly, I found myself having boldness and a strong desire to pray in my new language. Every time I prayed in this language, I felt faith arise. I felt passion, love, and a desire for God's beautiful laws. *The infilling of the Holy Spirit was so life-changing that my heart was overwhelmed with a desire to please my heavenly Father, to live for Jesus Christ His son, and to walk in the fullness of all that the Holy Spirit had for me.* Not long afterward, I began to hear the call to go to Bible college and make a radical career change away from engineering and into full-time ministry.

THE AHA MOMENT

In the summer of 1666, a young, soon-to-be scholar named Isaac Newton was sitting in his garden when, as the legend goes, he was hit on the head by a falling apple. The trajectory of the wayward fruit prompted an "aha moment" that resulted in the discovery of the law of gravity: "What goes up," Newton exclaimed, "must come down!" Now, did the law of gravity come into existence the moment Sir Isaac Newton was hit on the head? Of course not. The law had been in existence since the dawn of creation – Newton simply wasn't aware of the law. In the same way, God's ancient laws, His eternal ways, and His infallible truths had always been in play, but at that moment, I came into a radical, firsthand contact with them.

Maybe you've heard the saying, "You don't know what you don't know," or "What you don't know can't hurt you." I don't know if there's a bigger mistruth than that one. What I didn't know was not only hurting me; it was hindering me AND harming me. But thank God for the Holy Spirit, who leads us into all truth. As Jesus said in John 8:32, "You shall know the truth, and the truth shall make you free." Get ready for a new level of freedom as you step onto the pathway of truth. Freedom is God's desire for you, but it requires hearing the truth and then adhering to the truth.

The first two or three months of 2005 in San Diego were not easy. As we began to build a team, we were constantly bombarded by our city's culture. As I mentioned in the introduction, well-meaning people, even potential team members, told us that if we wanted to build a big church in San Diego, then there were three things we must not do.

#1. Whatever you do, do not move in the power of the Holy Spirit.

#2. Do not appoint women to any type of leadership, authority, influence, or position in the church.

#3. Do not speak about money. After all, this is Southern California, and the people here are materialistic. If you speak about their money, they will leave.

This was fantastic because it immediately identified the three areas of our culture that were in conflict with the kingdom of God, and I knew I needed to bring these down. I had discovered my assignment: to replace a worldly, infected culture with a life-changing and powerful kingdom culture that was established, rooted, and grounded in God's word and truth. We knew God had not sent us all the way from Sydney, Australia, to give San Diegans what they already had. We have not left everything behind to give California another helping of what was already here. We knew God knew what He was doing when He sent us here. He had not made a mistake. He was sending us to this city because he knew this city needed what He had fashioned into our DNA.

If you become like your city, you lose authority over your city. To influence a city for the kingdom of God, you must become an ambassador of heavenly truths. Heavenly realities are established through the planting of heavenly truths. These truths lie resident within his word. However, we are not just a word church; we are a

Spirit church. These two entities work powerfully together, just like we see in Genesis 1, where the Holy Spirit hovers over the face of the waters, and God says let there be light, and bam, light came! The Devil knows the level of power that is discharged when the Word and the Holy Spirit come into alignment.

When the Word and the Holy Spirit come into alignment, it shifts darkness and ushers in the light of heaven. We are called to overthrow the darkness with the light of the gospel, the light of the glory of God. We are called to be light bearers. Psalm 119:105 says, "Thy word is a lamp unto my feet and a light unto my path." Light resides in the word of God. The Devil knows in order to keep the world in darkness; he must resist, obstruct, and block the word of God from entering the earth. The Devil doesn't mind our TEDtalks or lectures. He doesn't mind our motivational speaking, but his fury is kindled when the word of God is preached.

GIFTS AND AUTHORITY

At Awaken Church, we believe some of God's greatest men are women. We believe every healthy home has a mother's voice and a father's voice. *We believe God not only speaks to women, but He can also speak through our women. We believe just like a healthy home, a healthy and vibrant church has both male and female preachers, teachers, and ministers of the word of God!* This is consistent with the entire New Testament, not to mention the Old Testament.

At Awaken Church, we believe God wants you to flourish and prosper. Psalm 24 says the earth is the Lord's and the fullness thereof. The entire universe belongs to God. God has given the entire world and its dominion into the hands of men. He wants you to exercise authority, He wants you to steward His resources and he wants you to walk in blessing, so He tests you with what is called the *tithe*. The tithe is the first 10 percent of your income, and He asks you to bring it to Him by way of honoring Him as being first in your life. Whenever you do this, you proclaim Him as king over your life. A king has two responsibilities: protection and provision. First, it is a king's responsibility to provide protection for the subjects of his kingdom. Second, it is a king's responsibility to bring provision to those within his kingdom. This is why it says in the book of Malachi that if we will bring our tithes into God's storehouse, He will open the windows of heaven and pour out blessings, provision, and he will rebuke the devourer for our sake, which is protection.

If God cannot trust you with the tithe, how can He trust you with more? The word tithe means 10th or test. God never tests us to fail us; He tests us to promote us. If you can't trust Him with your 10 percent, then God knows He can't trust you with more. This has been a powerful truth that I've discovered in my life as I honor God with the first fruits of all my income, as I began to give offerings over and above that, as I began to sow into His kingdom, and as I committed finances to the building of His house, Leanne and I have experienced unprecedented blessing and favor beyond our wildest dreams. When I left engineering to go to Bible college, my father told me in no uncertain terms that I was on my own. "Not one cent, not one cent!" he yelled at me as I pulled out of the driveway. And true to his word, not one cent of support did he afford us. But the Bible says if my mother and father forsake me, then the Lord will take care of me. This is exactly what Leanne and I have experienced. We have lived in three nations, serving God with all of our hearts, and we have experienced the supernatural overflow and provision of God's abundant grace and blessings in our lives. It is unmatched and unparalleled in the universe. There is no one like our God. At Awaken Church, we want you to enter into a brand-new expression of what it means to flourish, to prosper, and to bless and honor the one true God. Strap on your helmet, put on your seatbelt, and get ready to go where you've never gone before.

At Awaken Church, we know people need more than an entertaining word from one of our pastors. I'm not trying to belittle the revelation, the anointing, or the ministry gifting that our extraordinary team carries. But I do know this. When someone has been given six weeks to live because of terminal cancer, they need more than an entertaining homily. They need more than three points. They need an encounter with a life-changing, all-powerful God. We believe the same Jesus who walked the earth 2,000 years ago can live in us, with us, and through us when we allow the Holy Spirit to come upon us and fill us. You and I are never more like Jesus Christ than when we are full of the Holy Spirit.

In Acts 1:8, the resurrected Jesus told His followers, "You will receive power when the Holy Spirit comes on you." In John 14:12, He also told His followers, "Whoever believes in me will do the works I have been doing, and they will do even greater things than these, because I am going to the Father." Jesus said that when He went to the Father, He would send the Holy Spirit upon His followers. The church is called to be like Jesus Christ in the earth. Jesus healed the sick, raised the dead, cleansed the lepers, cast out demons, and performed many miracles, all through the power of the Holy Spirit. Without the Holy Spirit, Jesus did not perform one miracle. But through the Holy Spirit, He turned the world upside down. At Awaken Church, the Holy Spirit will fall upon you, and you will become a powerful you-version of Jesus Christ in the earth, to the glory of God the Father!

CHAPTER THREE

Awaken To A New Experience

FRESH, REAL, POWERFUL

"Behold, I will do a new thing, Now it shall spring forth; Shall you not know it? I will even make a road in the wilderness And rivers in the desert."
Isaiah 43:19 NKJV

I love new things. Every time I buy a new pair of shoes, pants, a cool jacket, a new car, a new surfboard, or a wetsuit, I can't wait to try it out and put it on. There's something beautiful about new. The scripture above in Isaiah 43:19 is a verse that Leanne and I received over and over again about what our church would be like in San Diego. I believe that Awaken Church is called to be exactly that: a river in the desert, a road in the wilderness, and a springing forth of God doing a new thing.

It's not that God needed to reinvent himself or that his truths had become outdated by a 21st-century, post-Christian era. Actually, it was more like the unchanging truth continually needs to be expressed through a new sound. God hates to be predictable. He is the Ancient of Days, which means that He never expires, grows old, or becomes outdated. *For the next billion years, we will still be blown away each and every day by the majesty, wonder, splendor, and awesomeness of our God!*

At Awaken Church, we want you to experience God in three specific ways: **FRESH, REAL, and POWERFUL!**

I can still remember the moment in July 2005 when I was driving in my car on the freeway from Del Mar to Solana Beach, having a conversation with the Lord. The Holy Spirit asked me, "Jurgen, what kind of church are you going to plant?" I began to tell him all about this church I had in my head, a church I thought would be really hip, cool, and contemporary. Halfway through my monologue, I realized God was not asking me because he wanted to know; He was asking me because he wanted to reveal. I said, "Forgive me, Lord. What kind of church do you want me to plant?" It was then that these three words came to me: fresh, real, and powerful!

1. FRESH

"Fresh" means the Word is not stale bread, not yesterday's revelation, not some secondhand, "old hat" principal or truth, but rather something fresh, straight from heaven. There are two words for the word "Word" in the Bible. The first one is the word logos, and the second is the word rhema. Logos means the written word, whereas rhema means the revealed word. Jesus uses both of these in his first temptation with the devil in the wilderness. After Jesus had fasted for 40 days, Matthew 4:4 records that the devil said to him, seeing that he was hungry, "If you are the son of God, command these stones to become bread!" Jesus responds, "It is written (logos) that man does not live by bread alone but by every word that proceeds from the mouth of God" (Rhema). We build our lives on what God has said – his laws, statutes, commands, edicts, and principles. However, we move forward on what God is saying. This is the Rhema activation of the word of God. It's the prophetic edge. Because God lives outside of time, his word is not relegated to or conditioned by time. His word is neither captured by nor limited by time. When God speaks, it is simultaneously historical, current, and prophetically futuristic.

Like God, Time is a Trinity: past, present, and future. God created time so that there would come a time when time would be no more. He did this in his manifold wisdom so that there would be an end to sin, suffering, disease, violence, oppression, injustice, and, most of all, death. That's why 1 Corinthians 15:55 says, "Where, oh death, is your victory? Where, oh death, is your sting? For death has been swallowed up in victory!" Because time is a Trinity – yesterday, today, tomorrow or past, present, future – God's word dominates all three of these landscapes. *A fresh word from heaven will operate in all three dimensions simultaneously; it will redeem your past, bring hope to your present, and provide magnificent vision and direction for your future.*

This is what is meant by fresh! I believe life is too short to listen quietly to a well-written but lifeless sermon or applaud a three-points-and-apoem homily describing an esoteric and ineffectual reflection of God's love. Life is too short to teach from old-school theology books that are completely irrelevant to our current culture and the needs of today. *If God doesn't expire, then neither should his word. It should always be fresh.*

2. REAL

One of the hallmarks of the 21st Century is a phenomenon in television known as reality TV. From the 50s to the 90s, people were content with scripted programs where fictitious characters faced fictional problems, overcoming them through fictional solutions! For example, MacGyver impressed me week after week with his fancy gadgets and ability to turn simple household things like a paper clip into a device that could disarm an atomic bomb. By the 21st Century, though, a generation plagued by uncertainty, disappointment, and the pain of divorce wanted something more from television viewing. They wanted to see real-life people in real-life scenarios facing real-life situations in real-life events. This was a prophetic moment for the church – if she was listening. The Holy Spirit was trying to show us that the world doesn't want to walk into our churches and hear another sermon, another theoretical theology of the afterlife, or another irrelevant geographical study of Middle Eastern nomadic tribes. The world is hungry for real-life answers to real-life problems that bring real-life solutions.

The world was asking the church, "Does the Bible have real answers to my real dilemmas? Does the Bible have real solutions to real problems? Can the Bible bring me into an encounter with a God who is real, or does faith simply mean living without any experiential proof whatsoever?" Fortunately, I do not know how to live a Christianity where the faith is simply a matter of blind belief, not backed up by any powerful, significant, and correlating experience. Rather, my experience is the exact opposite. When I read the Bible, I see the testimonies of men and women who stepped out on God's word, who trusted his voice and his guidance, who experienced the supernatural, the miraculous, the extraordinary, and amazing breakthroughs – all because they trusted and believed that God could be experienced. This is called "real."

The only way to give people a real encounter with God is to become real ourselves. Leanne and I have made it a personal principle that we will preach and teach from our life experiences. I once heard a great preacher say that if you will preach from your weaknesses, failures, and struggles, you will never run out of material! We have decided to "keep it real" in the pulpit. I remember a very powerful, life-changing moment in prayer with the Holy Spirit, where he said to me, "Jürgen, I no longer want you to practice what you preach…" Right there, I thought, "Hang on a minute; who is this? This can't be God, surely?" He then went on to say, "I want you to preach what you practice!" In other words, you apply it to your life first, and then you'll be able to teach others how to apply it to their lives. He showed me that when we preach things that we do not practice, we do not know the correct cadence, temperance, and grace to present that particular truth or principle. But when we first apply the word of God to our lives, we experience the challenge and sometimes the disappointment, but always the euphoria of his word operating in our lives. Then, and only then, will we have the right alchemy to preach it to others.

At Awaken Church, you will find that every series we preach tackles real-life issues, opening up the Scriptures to show how they still have the power to bring radical transformation, healing, redemption, hope, and power in every circumstance or situation that people are facing. We are not afraid to be real; in fact, Leanne and I quite often throw ourselves under the bus, and as our congregations laugh at some of the stupid mistakes that we have made, you can literally see them breathe a sigh of relief as if to say, "Wow, if they can make it, then I can make it too!" And I think that is exactly what God is looking for! I often revel in the Yelp reviews that comment negatively that we are "way too real" and nowhere near "religious" enough! LOL. I love this. Mission accomplished!

3. POWERFUL

Jesus said in Acts 1:8 that you shall receive power when the Holy Spirit comes upon you, and you will be my witnesses in Jerusalem, Judea, Samaria, and to the uttermost parts of the earth. The Bible also explains in Acts 10:38 how God anointed Jesus of Nazareth with the Holy Spirit and with power, and how "Jesus went about doing good and healing all who were oppressed of the devil, for God was with him!"

If a church gathering is not powerful, I have to ask the question: "Is God showing up?" I don't want to build a church where people can't experience the presence and the power of the living God. At Awaken Church, it is our mandate to bring people into an encounter with the power of the Holy Spirit. Every week, we see miracles, extraordinary healings, breakthroughs, and deliverances. This power flows from the combination of two sources: firstly, the word of God, and secondly, the Holy Spirit. At Awaken Church, we have made it our highest priority not to water down the preaching of God's truth, his Word. *We recognize that this commitment is not at all popular with modern culture, but we also recognize that modern culture has no power to deliver us from evil!* Instead, modern culture tells us that we should coexist, put up with, and accept living with all kinds of torment and affliction. This mentality is less than God's best for our lives!

Many times, my well-meaning friends and companions in the ministry have tried to encourage me to move away from ministering in the power of the Holy Spirit. They say that he is "weird," that he will freak people out, and that even though he is God, you cannot trust him. He will turn people away from God. Yes, I am being a bit facetious, but I'm trying to make a point. It simply is that stupid. The greatest asset to the building of your church is the presence of the person of the Holy Spirit. He is not a force, not a mist, not a formula. He is the third person of the Trinity, just like Jesus but invisible (don't misunderstand; when I say invisible, I don't mean he's not present, not able to be experienced. You had better believe that when the Holy Spirit turns up, the supernatural begins to flow).

The Bible teaches us that we face a supernatural foe, a supernatural enemy. Revelation 12:4 says that when the devil was cast out of heaven, he swept away a third of the angels with his tail, and these angels followed him down to the earth, being lured by the promise that on earth they would be the subjects who would receive worship, whereas, in heaven, they were the subjects who had to give worship. They have made it their quest to dominate and enslave men, forcing them to do their bidding. Men are gripped and brought into captivity by the evil one through their vices, their appetites, and their addictions. Men are snared by the lusts of these supernatural beings. However, through the power of the person of the Holy Spirit, he breaks every chain and removes every yoke, casting out all that is unclean and oppressive.

To fight a supernatural foe, you must have supernatural weaponry! This is what the Bible calls the gifts of the Holy Spirit. There are nine of these listed in 1 Corinthians 12 - 14. At Awaken Church, our DNA classes not only teach these gifts, but beginners on the journey receive these gifts, learning how to walk in them and seeing them in operation to bring supernatural results to supernatural problems!

You were created to walk with God. God is supernatural, paranormal. Therefore, as you walk with God, you will experience the supernatural and the paranormal. You do not need to fear evil because, as a son or daughter of the Most High God, you were created to conquer evil wherever it may raise its ugly head. You were created to exercise dominion over the earth, to subdue everything that opposes the one true God. In Genesis 1:28, the Bible says that after God created man, he blessed him and said, "Be fruitful and multiply, fill the earth, and subdue it, exercise dominion over the fish of the sea, the birds of the air, and the beasts of the field." *At Awaken Church, we do not preach a powerless Christianity but rather a powerful Christian experience. You were created to conquer, to overcome, to defeat every enemy, every work of darkness, and every demonic force that comes against you through the name that is above every other name, the name of Jesus!* To Him belongs all the glory and all the honor forever and ever, amen! So, don't fear the Holy Spirit, but rather allow yourself to awaken to a brand new encounter and reality with the third member of God's holy Trinity.

CHAPTER FOUR

Awaken To The Culture Clash

FAITH, HOPE, LOVE

In the Gospel of Mark, Chapter 6, Jesus comes to his hometown of Nazareth and begins to preach and proclaim his ministry, especially the miracles, healings, signs, and wonders taking place through Him. As the people listen to Him, the Bible says they became offended at Him, saying to one another, *"Is this not the carpenter's son? Are not his brothers James, Joses, and Jambres here with us, Are not his sisters and mother also?"* The Bible says they were offended at him, so much so that he could not do any mighty work there except that he laid his hands on a few sick people and healed them. The Bible says Jesus marveled at their unbelief. Jesus then said a prophet is not without honor, except in his own country and amongst his own brethren.

Imagine that! The Almighty God, Creator of the universe, comes to his hometown with a desire to perform miracles and operate in the supernatural, but his power is literally restricted from flowing because of the people's unbelief. Of all the things we can have Jesus marvel at in our lives, the one thing you don't want him marveling at is your lack of faith. Jesus desired to do something mighty, something powerful and miraculous, but their unbelief would not allow it to be so. *They had become so familiar with his humanity that they could not correctly discern his divinity.* All they could see was what they had known, 30 years of his past growing up in the house of Joseph, the local carpenter. They had no idea that this was more than a carpenter's son, that this was indeed the son of God, the Messiah, the chosen one, the savior of the entire world. He was here in their midst, performing signs and wonders in every single town, but when it came to their town, he could do no mighty work because of their unbelief. What a sad scripture.

Faith releases the power of God, while doubt and disbelief shut it down. The Devil knows this, and that is why he is relentless in his attack on the word of God. He doesn't want it taught in our schools, he doesn't want it proclaimed in our halls of justice or courtrooms, he doesn't want it in our colleges, and he certainly does his best to water it down in our pulpits. There is a law, according to the rabbis, called "the law of first mentions." This means the first time something appears in Scripture; the phrasing denotes its character or influence throughout the rest of the Scriptures. Satan is introduced in the Bible as the serpent who poses the question, "Has God really said? Can God really be trusted?" Even Jesus said, "When I return to the earth, will I find faith in the earth?" Words shape culture, and culture shapes society. Things thrive or die in a culture.

For many, many years, I heard teachings about sowing and reaping. The teachings went along these lines: If you put good seed in good soil, you get a good harvest. But that's not necessarily true. I can take the best orange seeds out of Florida and plant them in the rich and fertile soil of North Dakota, but I ain't going to get any oranges. Why? Because the culture, atmosphere, and environment (the weather conditions) are not suitable for citrus fruits. So, my efforts would be null and void. There's nothing wrong with the seed, and likewise, there's nothing wrong with the soil, but there was everything wrong with the atmosphere for growing citrus.

In the same way, the Kingdom of God, also known as the Kingdom of Heaven, thrives in a certain atmosphere or culture. The Devil knows this to be true, so he works to create a culture and an atmosphere that is anathema to the Kingdom of God. To be clear, God moves in atmospheres. At Awaken Church, our goal each week is to try to emulate the atmosphere of heaven here on earth. If we can accomplish this, we will see heavenly results here on earth. The earth is never more like heaven than when it is worshiping. Worship is an intrinsic part of our weekly expression in our services. Worship sets the tone; it's the thermostat that changes the temperature to match Heaven's culture. Many times, before we even get to the preaching, people are already experiencing God, being healed, set free, and delivered. God moves in an atmosphere of faith, so we must preach messages overflowing with faith.

1 Corinthians 13, known as the love chapter, discusses *"three things that remain."* After all is said and done, when all the noise settles down, the Bible teaches us that three things will outlast all things: faith, hope, and love. If you were to ask me what the culture of heaven on earth would look like, I would say it's a culture of faith, hope, and love! This is the culture where God moves powerfully in people's lives. This is the atmosphere, an environment that causes human beings to thrive, to awaken to their God potential, their God dreams, and their God given destiny. Let's look at each atmosphere individually, as each contains powerful ingredients.

FAITH

Faith is not just believing that God can; it is believing that God will. Faith is always rooted in the word of God. Romans 10:17 says faith comes by hearing and hearing by the word of God. Upon hearing the word of God, faith rises in our spirits, and we begin to believe for the impossible; we begin to reach for the unseen and step into the unknown. *All progress is dependent upon faith. Faith is the key that unlocks the treasuries of heaven. Faith is the conduit through which the power of God flows from heaven to earth.* Hebrews 11 tells us it is by faith that the heroes of old saw God perform amazing miracles in the earth. The Bible teaches us that God has not changed, and even though these men of God are now seated in glory, we can now operate in the same faith as them and see God do the same miracles in our generation. *But make no mistake, the world in which you and I live is governed by a Satanic spirit that hates faith and erodes faith because it knows faith is the landing strip where the power of God and miracles can land on the earthly realm.* Every miracle brings glory to God. That is why there is such a war on faith.

HOPE

Hebrews 11 says faith is the substance of things hoped for, the evidence of things unseen. This means that faith springs out of hope. Where there is no hope, there is no faith. *Hope is the soil that allows faith to thrive.* The book of Romans says God is the God of hope. Hope, in its most fundamental definition, is the belief that tomorrow will be better than today. Hope is always future-centered. Sadly, many in our generation have lost all hope; therefore, they have given up on a bright future. When God created mankind, He put our eyes in the front of our heads for a reason: We are meant to be looking forward because, by definition, looking forward is hoping.

My children always look forward to Christmas and birthdays because they hope to be showered with gifts, presents, and generous benevolence. Your Heavenly Father wants you to live with hope. Hope is rooted and grounded in the promises of God. Did you know there are so many promises in Scripture that you could believe God for ten different promises every day for an entire year?

When people walk into Awaken Church, one of the first things we want to awaken in them is a sense of hope. We want you to know that your best days are in front of you, not behind you. We want you to know that your greatest days are yet to come and that the God that you have encountered is a God who redeems your past, breaks every chain, loses every cord, heals, delivers, and restores. At Awaken Church, we take great delight in getting your hope switch turned on!

Sadly, many people have given up on hope, clinging to the wounds of disappointment, betrayal, and discouragement. The Bible does say that hope deferred makes the heart sick. However, the God we serve is one who heals our broken hearts, and He is not a man that He should lie. Most people have lost hope because their hope was in the words of the promises of men. Maybe it was a father who said he would never leave the mother or a mother who promised she would always be there. Perhaps it was the betrayal of a spouse, an infidelity, or a deep wounding. That is why Jesus Christ heals the brokenhearted – so that our heart can hope once again. You were created to hope. Look at this powerful scripture Jesus read in the temple in Luke Chapter 4:

The Spirit of the Lord is upon me, because he has anointed me to preach good news to the poor. He has sent me to heal the broken hearted, to proclaim liberty to the captives and recovery of sight to the blind, to sit at liberty those who are oppressed, and to proclaim the year of the Lord's favor.

Did you notice the order? First, He preaches good news; this is where our hope is anchored, but the soil must be clean of impediments for hope to grow. That's why the next part of the verse says He heals the brokenhearted. Once our heart is healed, we are no longer captive to the wounds and betrayals of our past. Then and only then are we able to see, hence recovery of sight to the blind. Now that we have vision flowing from hope, we can begin to find freedom and a declarative proclamation that God is favorable. At Awaken Church, we seek to preach the good news, heal the brokenhearted, set the captives free, restore vision to our lives, bring liberty and expansion, and declare the greatness of God.

LOVE

Without love, nothing flourishes. The Bible says God is love. The Bible says we are made by God; therefore, we are made by love for love. It is the search for love that will cause a young woman to get caught in the web of promiscuity and broken sexuality. A longing for love will cause human beings to do the most desperate and sometimes the most despicable things. Whatever is loved thrives when it receives that love. Just like flowers thrive when it rains, they will also dry up and wither if sheltered or blocked from the rain. They need to receive the rain that falls from the heavens in the same way our hearts and our souls need to drink in the love that falls and flows from our Heavenly Father. If everybody in the world received the love of God and walked in the love of God, crime would be a thing of the past. We would have no more murderers, rapists, or thieves. People would no longer lie, cheat, and steal. This is why heaven is such a magnificent place, because all of us will be experiencing the love of God, and, at the same time, we will be transmitters of that love to one another. That's why I believe we can have heaven on earth if we simply walk in God's love and laws. Don't even get me started on how little we would pay in taxes because we wouldn't need police or government to make stringent and restrictive laws. This is what the Apostle Paul taught about love. You will notice that this is the most often read piece of Scripture at weddings and funerals.

Though I speak with the tongues of men and angels but have not love, I have become sounding brass or a clanging cymbal. And though I have the gift of prophecy, and understand all mysteries and all knowledge, and though I have all faith, so that I could remove mountains, but have not love, I am nothing. And though I bestow all my goods to feed the poor, and though I give my body to be burned, but have not love, it profits me nothing. Love never fails. But whether there are prophecies, they will fail; whether there are tongues, they will cease; whether there is knowledge, it will vanish away. But when that which is perfect has come, then that which is in part will be done away. When I was a child, I spoke as a child, I understood as a child, I thought as a child; but when I became a man, I put away childish things. For now we see in a mirror, dimly, but then face to face. Now I know in part, but then I shall know just as I also am known. And now abide faith, hope, love, these three; but the greatest of these is love."

I Corinthians 13:1-3, 8, 10-13 NKJV

Jesus said by this will all men know that you are my disciples: if you have love for one another. He didn't say, "If you perform miracles," he didn't say, "If you walk on water," he didn't say, "If you feed the multitude with only a few loaves and a couple of fish." He said, "All people will know you are my disciples if you love one another." This means that truly loving one another is one of the most challenging of all human expressions! Love keeps no record of wrong, yet my heart wants to chalk up every offense and violation and hold you accountable.

Love forgives, love lets go, love believes the best, love hopes all things, love never leaves, and love never gives up. Satan has created a culture in this world where hate reigns and, like a Pac-Man, consumes love. Love has become a scarce commodity. The world is confused about the true definition of love. I was driving on the freeway recently, and the car in front of me had a bumper sticker that said, "Love is a German Shepherd." The band Foreigner sang a song entitled "I Want to Know What Love Is." We are called to show the world what real love looks like. Did you know the word "love" is not mentioned anywhere in the Koran? Only in the Holy Scriptures, the Bible, does it teach us that our God is a loving God and that He so loved us that He gave His only begotten son for us. Love goes first; love sacrifices; love pays the price personally to benefit others. That's what love looks like. Love changes the world. When humans wither and wilt, it is always due to a lack of love.

At Awaken Church, you will discover the love of God, but we will not reduce that discovery to an exclusively cognitive ascent. You will also experience God's love firsthand in the atmosphere and culture that's created. Our mission, or mandate, if you will, is to overthrow the cultures of our world that are hostile to the culture of the kingdom of heaven (faith, hope, and love) so that we can see people experiencing heaven right here on earth.

CHAPTER FIVE

Awaken To A New Mission

CONNECT, DEVELOP, EMPOWER

"With great power comes great responsibility!"
"You will be like a god to them..."
"I realized this was my purpose in life!"
"You are the chosen one!"
"You were supposed to destroy the Sith, not join them!"

Hollywood blockbuster movies are filled with anecdotes for the central drive of human beings – PURPOSE! You were created on purpose for a purpose. One of the great and most damaging lies of the last century is the premise that the theory of Evolution espouses, namely that "YOU came from NOTHING, YOU are going NOWHERE, and there is absolutely NO MEANING OR PURPOSE to your life." Fortunately, anyone with even the slightest heart for truth can see the incompatibility with reality that this pseudo-science attempts to prop up! Intelligent design floods both the macro and micro universe around us, not to mention the vast and infinite complexities of the human biological structure.

Your new phone (Android or iPhone) exists because it was created to "serve a purpose." The chair you're sitting on exists because someone designed it to "serve a purpose." This is true for EVERYTHING you see, your toothbrush – purpose. Your car – purpose. Your deodorant – purpose. In fact, the ONLY reason it exists is because the Creator of it wanted it to fulfill a purpose. Perhaps the GREATEST realization I have come to since my salvation is that God created you with a distinct purpose in mind.

"I know the plans that I have for you, says the LORD..." Jeremiah 29:11

"Before I formed you in the womb, I knew you. Before you were born I sanctified you and ordained you a prophet to the nations!" Jeremiah 1:3

Before you were born, God had a plan and a design for your life. They say there are two great days in a person's life; day number one was the day you were born. Day number two was the day you discovered WHY!

At AWAKEN Church, we know the most important thing for a human being is to discover their purpose, identity, and destiny. We accomplish this through our DNA Course:

CONNECT. DEVELOP. EMPOWER.

As you walk through our DNA Course, you will begin to discover three magnificent treasures:

1. You will discover who God is: His inexhaustible love for you and His priceless plan of salvation that He paid for your life.
2. You will discover who YOU are: every day, people look in the mirror thinking they see themselves. Sadly, though, you can't discover who you are from a mirror; all a mirror can do is show you your reflection. You will NEVER truly discover who you are until you look into the face of God and His Word, because the Bible says you were created in His image and in His likeness. (Genesis 1:27)
3. You will discover WHY you are here: your life has a meaning, a purpose, a destiny. God did not make a mistake when it came to you being here. YOU are meant to be here, and God has a significant and unique plan for your life.

Let's look at the essentials of the DNA Course:

CONNECT

Have you ever sat in an airport or a coffee shop that promised WIFI only to discover that the connection is either painfully slow or altogether non-existent? It's extraordinarily frustrating! It's the same with life. Believe it or not, God created you for connections. In fact, one of the first commentaries God made after creating man was that it was NOT GOOD for man to be ALONE! Humans work better when they are connected. Science proves this again and again. When we are around other people, our endorphin release increases and we become happier and brighter people. We are rich when surrounded by people with whom we can share our lives. We are poor when we have no one to share our lives with. The science behind this is irrefutable. That's why when we punish people for doing wrong or committing crimes, we often place them in solitary confinement. Isolation is punishment.

One of the greatest marketing ploys today is that of social media, where the folks at Google, Facebook, Twitter, Instagram, and Snapchat get rich by exploiting the human craving and need for connection. They KNOW that their platforms do not ACTUALLY create meaningful connections; they create a pseudo-connection, a hollow image of meaningful relationships. You may have hundreds of friends on Facebook but nobody to call in a crisis.

As Proverbs 27:7 says, *"A satisfied soul loathes the honeycomb, but to a hungry person every bitter thing tastes sweet!"* People do not even realize they are consuming a counterfeit connection through social media because they are so hungry for ANY connection.

The largest organ in the human body is the skin. It is filled with trillions of nerve endings because it longs for touch. A hug, a squeeze of the shoulder, a pat on the back, or a kiss on the cheek sends the endorphins in your brain into an overload. You and I need connection. As humans, we THRIVE in community. Throughout the ages, people were grouped into tribes, families, nations, and nationalities—our sense of identity, worth, and belonging was born from these origins. However, the day you were "born again," you became part of the family of God. As you connect, you will find people of similar ilk who will do life with you, pray with you, and share strengths and struggles with you. This is so important.

"Two are better than one; they have a good reward for their labor. If either of them falls down, one can help the other up. But pity anyone who falls and has no one to help them up. Also, if two lie down together, they will keep warm. But how can one keep warm alone? Though one may be overpowered, two can defend themselves. A cord of three strands is not easily broken."
Ecclesiastes 4:9-11

Remember, the wolf, the lion, and every predator go after the lone, isolated sheep. Don't allow the devil to isolate you. Get connected. Your life will AWAKEN to a whole new sense of worth and meaning.

DEVELOP

The saddest potential is the "never" developed potential. As the poet John Greenleaf Whittier once said, "Of all sad words of tongue or pen, the saddest is these: 'It might have been.'" I will never forget the time a few years ago when I had the privilege of driving with my hero, Pastor Tommy Barnett. We were talking about all things ministry related, and I was trying to do the delicate dance of assessing how many questions were too many questions. I wanted him to like me and enjoy my company, but I also didn't want to miss out on getting advice from this extraordinary human being about life, ministry, impact, influence, and a host of other topics.

Halfway through an answer he was giving me on developing and raising leaders, Pastor Tommy asked me a question: "What do you think is the richest place in the city? Where do you think the most treasure lies?" It caused me great pause. I wanted to impress my newfound mentor, so I said, "The banks? It's got to be the banks! That's where all the money is. Without banks, we can't get the funding to build our buildings and reach our city." But Pastor Tommy shook his head and suggested I take another guess. Slightly embarrassed, I thought this would be my redemption moment. I would surely get it right this time. Think, think, think: Where is the richest place in a city where the most treasure lies? Just then, we came upon a bend, and Pastor Tommy pulled over. He said, "Right there," and he pointed to a graveyard.

Somewhat gobsmacked, I didn't want to reveal my complete ignorance, but apparently, the puzzled expression on my face was as evident as a neon billboard in Vegas. Pastor Tommy said, "There is so much buried treasure here of men and women who died with their dreams, their potential, their gifting still inside them, having never developed and deployed them, having never truly lived." He said, "In every city, the graveyards hold the most buried treasure of lives that could have been... should have been... but never were. They died with their divine spark, their treasure, still within them."

At AWAKEN Church, our DNA Course is intended to serve as "divine potential mines" – helping each person discover the gold they have within, perhaps buried by layers of dirt and rubble. Life has a way of burying the divine spark, the greatness inside each of us. Disappointment, abandonment, abuse, neglect, childhood illness, divorce, and a myriad of other issues can bury the treasure that lies within. Discipleship is the brushing away of dirt in order to reveal the gold beneath. Sadly, some people try to hide their dirt, paint their dirt, or pretend they don't have any dirt. Others are too proud or perhaps too ashamed to let another person point out the dirt or ask for help removing the dirt. However, discipleship can only happen when we humble ourselves to allow others to help us deal with the dirt that is keeping the treasure buried.

At AWAKEN Church, we know everything that comes out of the ground doesn't come out ready to go but needs to be developed and processed. In the same way, we seek to develop the gold and the treasure inside each person, to AWAKEN them to their potential and, even more, to AWAKEN them to DREAM again. I know that sounds like an oxymoron, a contradiction of terms, but it's more than just a clever juxtaposition; it's a real truth. When I was awoken to the reality of God's hand upon me and the truth that He has placed gifts and callings within me, I awakened. At that moment,

I began to DREAM. The dream God has for you is always in line with the gifting and anointing He has placed within and upon your life! You may not see or even be aware of them, but don't worry. The Bible gives us a great little formula to unlock our awareness. It's in Psalm 37:4: "Delight yourself in the LORD and he will give you the desires of your heart!"

As you delight yourself in God, a divine transaction takes place, simultaneously purifying and revealing the desires of your heart. This then begins to expose the gifting in your life, gifts that are often lying dormant, abused, or simply misused. Now, a divine alignment begins to take place. As a young man, I was trained to be a mechanical engineer, but the truth is that I hated it. Getting up and going to work was a chore, but not knowing any better, I had resigned myself to believe "this is life." To get a home and be able to marry and raise a family, you have to work, so I figured this was just what people do. BUT... I had just gotten radically saved. Jesus had become my delight above everything else, and I began to see that I loved drama, I loved humor, I loved entertaining people (I was getting in trouble almost daily at my engineering job, where my desire to make people laugh was exacerbated by a captive audience of 24,000 employees. It was too much temptation to resist. I just thank God nobody died from any of my practical jokes. Yikes!)

I knew I loved people – I always had, my entire childhood. But I thought, "You can't exactly make a living out of loving people, entertaining them with stories and drama! Who's going to pay you to do that?" Well, little did I know that week by week, as I attended Wollongong Church of Christ (where I met my beautiful Leannie), God would begin peeling away the layers of dirt and revealing the call within. Once discovered, I kissed engineering goodbye and went off to Power Ministry School (PMS for short – no, really), which is known today as Hillsong College.

The next two years would be a hybrid cocktail of having my butt and behavior whooped and having truckloads of dirt exposed and removed from my heart and life. But it would all be painted with words affirming the call and potential within. God was developing me. He still hasn't stopped developing me. I never want Him to stop. I never want to take Satan's bait that I have arrived, and there is no more gold buried in the soil of my heart. The signature of God is a changed life. Let him develop all that He placed within you before you were conceived in your mother's womb!

EMPOWER

At AWAKEN Church, we believe God calls us to live a life beyond our human capacity, intellect, and experience. Because of this desire, He calls us not to frustration but to an impartation of POWER! Acts 1:6-8 says, "Therefore, when they had come together, they asked Him, saying, 'Lord, will You at this time restore the kingdom to Israel?' And He said to them, 'It is not for you to know times or seasons which the Father has put in His own authority. But you shall receive power when the Holy Spirit has come upon you, and you shall be witnesses to Me in Jerusalem, and in all Judea and Samaria, and to the end of the earth.'"

In this verse, the disciples were asking for details about the end times, and Jesus was basically saying, "Guys, you're not going to sit around and observe it happening; you're going to be EMPOWERED to BE the happening!" At AWAKEN, you will become aware of the POWER available to you to live over and above your expectations.

The Holy Spirit is the EMPOWERER. He is the third person of the Godhead, the Trinity. He comes upon us and fills us to overflowing so that we begin to speak in languages unlearned by our past. Through the Holy Spirit, you will enter into a realm where you can speak in the tongues of men and of angels (see 1 Corinthians 13), a realm where wisdom beyond your years begins to become an available reservoir for you. The power to be just like Jesus now wells up within you! In Matthew 10:1, Jesus gave his disciples a foretaste of what was to come. He sent them out to preach and proclaim the good news of the kingdom of God, heal the sick, raise the dead, cleanse lepers, and cast out demons. Jesus NEVER asks us to do something that he doesn't EQUIP and RESOURCE us to do. That is called EMPOWERING!

At AWAKEN Church, we believe God has a higher and greater plan and purpose for your life, one that requires His supernatural infilling and empowering to fulfill. The Holy Spirit did not come to make you weird; He came to make you POWERFUL and FRUITFUL. When He comes, He brings with Him nine distinct gifts. These gifts are evident expressions (think more like nine facets of the Holy Spirit's personality) operating through your life. They reveal WHO he is. He distributes words of WISDOM, words of KNOWLEDGE, discernment of SPIRITS, tongues, interpretation of tongues, and prophecy. He deposits a Spirit of FAITH (to do the impossible or miraculous), gifts (plural) of healing, and the working of miracles! As if Jesus wasn't already more than enough and so much more than we deserve, God also blesses us with this kind of gifted POWER to live life over and above what you may have previously imagined!

The goal of an EMPOWERED life is to AWAKEN you to the possibility that Ephesians 3:20 can become your reality: "Now to Him who is able to do exceedingly, abundantly above all that we can ask or think according to his power that is at work in us." Wow, what an abundant life awaits us as we surrender to the infilling presence of the person of the Holy Spirit. Don't just get connected, don't just get developed, get EMPOWERED! Empowering is activating. Your fully charged phone must be turned on for it to be a blessing to you. Its applications must be activated for you to fully experience and enjoy all they can do. In the same way, you and I need to be "activated" into our gifting and callings. This is being empowered!

Let me let you in on a little kingdom secret I have discovered over the years:

THE LEVEL TO WHICH YOU WILL HUMBLE YOURSELF AND SURRENDER TO GOD AND HIS LEADERSHIP IN YOUR LIFE IS THE LEVEL TO WHICH HIS POWER WILL FLOW THROUGH YOU!

Don't let the devil make you fearful and hold you back from fully surrendering. Jesus gave himself fully over to God to save us, so He is our example that we can fully and completely trust God!

CHAPTER SIX

Awaken Divine Flows

HEALING, FRUITFULNESS, PROSPERITY

"Then Isaac sowed in that land, and reaped in the same year a hundredfold; and the LORD blessed him. The man began to prosper, and continued prospering until he became very prosperous; for he had possessions of flocks and possessions of herds and a great number of servants. So the Philistines envied him. Now the Philistines had stopped up all the wells which his father's servants had dug in the days of Abraham his father, and they had filled them with earth. And Abimelech said to Isaac, 'Go away from us, for you are much mightier than we.' Then Isaac departed from there and pitched his tent in the Valley of Gerar, and dwelt there. And Isaac dug again the wells of water which they had dug in the days of Abraham his father, for the Philistines had stopped them up after the death of Abraham. He called them by the names which his father had called them. Also Isaac's servants dug in

the valley, and found a well of running water there. But the herdsmen of Gerar quarreled with Isaac's herdsmen, saying, 'The water is ours.' So he called the name of the well Esek, because they quarreled with him. Then they dug another well, and they quarreled over that one also. So he called its name Sitnah. And he moved from there and dug another well, and they did not quarrel over it. So he called its name Rehoboth, because he said, 'For now the LORD has made room for us, and we shall be fruitful in the land.'"
Genesis 26:12-22 NKJV

  Isaac was walking in his father's footsteps, quite literally. God appeared to Abram in Genesis 12 and asked him to leave his family, his country, and all that was familiar to him to sojourn and walk upon a land that God would give to Abram's descendants. At this stage, Abram did not even have one descendant; his wife Sarai was unable to conceive because she was barren. Now, almost a century later, Isaac is living in the land with his father's flocks and herds, and there is a battle over wells, the source of water. All life is sustained by water. Without it, everything dies: plants, animals, humans. Abraham, Isaac's father, had dug many wells to sustain the lives of his flock, herds, and family; however, the present occupants of the land were most unwilling to make room for what God had promised Abraham, let alone just "give it over" to him and his descendants. So, they stopped up the wells, filling in every well Abraham had dug. They knew that if they cut off the water supply, they cut off the supply of life. There is an age-old principle that says, *"Whatever you feed grows, and whatever you starve dies!"*

Isaac had to "dig again" the wells of his father, Abraham. The current occupants of the promised land were resistant, and they fought with Isaac over each and every breakthrough. Every time Isaac and his servants discovered water, the enemy came to take it away by claim. They were the original "claim jumpers"! Isaac models for us what persistence looks like: hard work, endurance, and breakthrough were all met with hostile resistance and warfare. Yet, Isaac knew this was his land of promise. All he had to do was NOT give up on his breakthrough, not give up on God coming through, which allows the enemy to attain victory through discouragement! So, he "dug again," and this time, the enemy was silenced. He had overcome Esek, meaning bitterness, and Sitnah, which means contention. God made room for him, and he called the place Rehoboth, which means wide places or streets. "God has made room for us," Isaac declared. Don't give up after you encounter hostility and opposition. Don't get bitter. Keep digging. Don't allow yourself to become worn out by the attrition of discouragement through the "contentions" of the devil warring against you and God's plans for your life. Keep digging, and you will find your Rehoboth!

In the summer of 2005, we began the church known today as AWAKEN Church. For seven years, we warred as we wandered the land God had promised. I knew we were to be one church in four locations. We had been told that it was nearly impossible to get a building in San Diego, that there existed NO ZONING for churches, and that the city was unwilling to give up its much-coveted tax revenues and income. On top of that, it was in the top five most expensive cities for commercial real estate in the USA. Seven years later, we purchased our first property in Carlsbad, CA, which would become a second campus, as our main congregation was in the Carmel Valley, CA, area. I had no idea that Carmel means "God's Vineyard" at the time, but we were learning how to grow fruitful vines and produce a new wine, God's wine, in the city of San Diego. We were becoming a fresh, new vintage with bold flavors, a smooth and delicate bouquet, accentuated with light and fruity hints of blackberries, and... Okay, I'm getting carried away, but you get the meaning. We were called to produce something new in this city, not give it the old wine of lifeless religion, but to bring a life-giving encounter that AWAKENS the soul. God's word and God's precious Holy Spirit do exactly that: bring life from the dead, even when it seems all hope is gone.

By 2013, we had now secured our central campus, a 34,000-square-foot building in central San Diego. God then asked us to fast for 40 days, and the word that came was, *"I want you to dig again the wells of your father Abraham!"* It was a weird word, to say the least, and I had NO IDEA what that meant. But God showed me that just like Abraham, who had in generations prior to Isaac dug wells, so too there were wells in California that the Abrahams (Christian patriarchs and statesmen) had dug in the generations before us, and that these wells were now "stopped up" by the enemy and no longer flowing. There were THREE wells that God showed me that He desired and had designated specifically to flow in our church: HEALING, FRUITFULNESS, and PROSPERITY.

1. HEALING

America had broken through in these three areas because her foundation had been set on the secure rock, the foundation of Jesus Christ and His word. While the rest of the world clung to religious traditions and the convenient tenets of the Christian faith, early American pulpits were aflame with preachers of righteousness, revivals of salvations accompanied by deliverances, healings, and miracles. America had virtue and faith in God, His word, and His church, and God had blessed that, and she sent healing evangelists worldwide, seeing souls saved and the most extraordinary miracles taking place. Kathryn Kuhlman, TL and Daisy Osborne, Maria Woodworth Etter, Benny Hinn, and many, many others were turning the world upside down and seeing Jesus Christ's healing power flow to a new generation.

Healing was a well that the enemy had been determined to stop up; however, as we fasted, we began to see a spring of supernatural healing flow in our church. Church is NOT meant to be just a building that sits on the intersection of two streets, a building that christens our babies, conducts our weddings, and buries our deceased. We are meant to be a house of the miraculous, a place where the healing power of Jesus can flow. There isn't one week that passes in our church where there isn't some amazing miracle or supernatural phenomena. We love seeing "terminal" get terminated when Jesus Christ's power disintegrates cancer, tumors, and disease. AWAKEN Church is more than a place of instruction, teaching, and preaching God's word; it's also a place where healing power flows like a spring.

Jesus paid for our healing by His stripes. He bears the receipt of your healing – it has been fully purchased and paid for. You don't have to beg; you just have to receive by getting into the flow. Psalm 103 says,

"Bless the LORD oh my soul, and all that is in me bless his holy name. Bless the LORD oh my soul and forget not all His benefits, who forgives all your iniquities, who heals all your diseases, who crowns you with loving kindness and redeems your life from destruction!"

He forgives ALL your iniquities, and He heals ALL your diseases. Not most, not some – the Word says ALL! Again, the scriptures say in ACTS 10:38 that *"God anointed Jesus of Nazareth with the Holy Spirit and with power, who went about doing good and healing all who were oppressed by the devil, for God was with Him!"*

It's easy for people to form incorrect theology while in a church where there has been no flow of power; you'll find yourselves believing things that don't line up with the scriptures. Now, to be sure, the scriptures show us what CAN be possible because they reflect God's will on the earth. These precious promises are activated through faith. Faith has an atmosphere that it creates and operates in. When we as humans want to go into outer space, we must take our 'atmosphere' with us; when we want to go deep sea diving, we can only do so if we take our atmosphere with us. We cannot survive underwater or in space without our atmosphere being present with us.

In the same way, heaven has an atmosphere in which it operates. Our job is to overthrow the atmosphere set by the evil one in the culture and create an atmosphere where God dwells in victory. Then, we see God's victorious power to heal, set free, and deliver, overcoming all the powers of darkness!

2. FRUITFULNESS

From "barren" to "fruitful" was the second spring that would FLOW through AWAKEN Church. As you begin to read the Bible, you discover that God's most favorite miracle is bringing fruitfulness where barrenness had previously reigned. People who could not conceive, who were barren, receive breakthrough and bring forth a son of promise. We see this throughout both the Old and the New Testaments, and it seems to be a state that is most common after the fall of man. In fact, it is the most consistent miracle that God performs. Barrenness exists in a world divorced from and devoid of God. He is the source of life and fruitfulness, and as people come into our church, they come into a FLOW where curses are broken, wombs are opened, and what was once unfruitful breaks forth and begins to produce!

AT AWAKEN Church, we know there is a flow that turns what was barren and desolate into what is fruitful and flourishing! "Sing Oh Barren" is the charge given by the LORD through the prophet Isaiah to a barren woman and barren land! Isaiah 54:1 says, *"Sing, O barren, thou that didst not bear; break forth into singing, and cry aloud, thou that didst not travail with child: for more are the children of the desolate than the children of the married wife, saith Jehovah."*

As she begins to sing, breakthrough begins to flow, and barrenness is overthrown, yielding to fruitfulness. But what does she sing? Definitely NOT the barren lament on the radio or the top 40 charts of this fallen, broken world! She begins to sing praises to God. Praise causes the spring of heaven to flow in our lives. We are a mirror reflection of heaven when we are praising our God.

There are 12 tribes in Israel; one was the most fruitful and largest. Can you guess which one? Judah. What does the name "Judah" mean? It means PRAISE! As you praise, strength comes. As you praise, breakthrough comes. Heaven's spring begins to flow toward your life, and barren, desolate voids begin to conceive. Once acidic soil now welcomingly receives seed and begins to produce fruitfulness!

Imagine owning the responsibility of land, its care and maintenance, fencing and upkeep, property taxes and other expenses, and the land not being productive for you. This is the pathway to poverty and bankruptcy. Conversely, imagine that land being so fertile and fruitful that you are producing one hundred times per annum all that is going out. That is called blessed and prosperous. That is what God wants your life to look like. One of my favorite miracles at AWAKEN Church is the amount of baby boys and girls I get to hug, kiss, and watch grow up – babies that, according to medical science, would never be here. Yet here they are! Not because of the hand of man, but because of the power of God!

One of my favorite movie scenes of all time is in the DreamWorks movie Prince of Egypt. God appears to Moses at a burning bush (or so the story goes in the book of Exodus), but when I first watched the scene in this movie, I felt that Spielberg and the team had really dropped the ball on detail in this scene. Rather than a BUSH with foliage burning, there is a flimsy, leafless stick smoldering. The shot then pans to Moses having a dialogue with God, whose presence is residing upon this bush, but each time the bush is pictured, it becomes more lush, until the very last scene where the bush is full of leaves, full of ripe fruit – so ripe, in fact, that the fruit is falling to the ground. God had momentarily let His presence reside on this dead tree, and LIFE flowed. This is what the Spirit of God does when we allow Him and His presence to reside in our lives.

After David was crowned King of Israel, he wanted to bring God's presence to Jerusalem, the capital of Israel. But there was a mishap on the way. The ARK of God, where His presence dwelt between the cherubim, was placed onto the back of a cart drawn by oxen instead of carried on the shoulders of priests. God does not follow behind what we call strength on the earth (oxen). He is the first and should be honored. Uzzah, one of the drivers of the ark, reaches out his hand to steady the ark and is struck dead for his error. David is mad at God and fearful for his own life and His household. It seems God is not at all able to be boxed in or housed by men. So, they choose a man who can take the ark to his house until they decide what to do with it! They choose Obed Edom the Gittite.

Obviously, the ark just killing Uzzah tells us that they don't really hold Obed Edom's life in high regard (his name means "servant of Edom/Esau," and he is from the Philistine city of Gath). The Bible says that Obed Edom takes the ark home, and for the next three months, instead of His children being struck dead or plagues and judgments breaking out, the Bible says that EVERYTHING in His house is blessed. Everything becomes so fruitful that the king hears about this and summons the ark, bringing it to Jerusalem correctly this time – on the shoulders of priests, not on a cart behind animals. If you follow Obed Edom and his kids, they become doorkeepers in the house of God for generations. A 3-month stint with God's presence changed their entire family line. They fell in love with God's presence. Nothing they had seen or experienced until that point compared with the fruitfulness of God's presence.

This is what we want for every person that comes into AWAKEN Church! Get ready to go from barren and unproductive to fruitful!

3. PROSPERITY

"Then Isaac sowed in that land and reaped in the same year a hundredfold; and the LORD blessed him. The man began to prosper, and continued prospering until he became very prosperous; for he had possessions of flocks and possessions of herds and a great number of servants. So the Philistines envied him..." Genesis 26:12-14

Did you see the progression in the above verses? Isaac began to PROSPER; he continued PROSPERING until he became VERY PROSPEROUS! Isaac is an example of what our lives should look like when we come to Christ, obey God, trust Him, and step out in faith. If God was so "anti-prosperity," as so many false teachers proclaim, then why is the Bible full of verses like this? PROSPERITY is the result of God's healing power flooding over your life, turning what was BARREN into FRUITFULNESS, and now you find yourself flourishing (PROSPERING!). To prosper means "to have an abundance beyond your needs." To be in poverty means "to have insufficient resources to meet your needs!" Don't be fooled or deceived; God wants you to prosper so that you can be a blessing and help to others!

The Bible says in Galatians 3: 13 that "Jesus became a curse to redeem those of us from under the curse, as it is written cursed is any man that is hanged on a tree, so that the blessing of Abraham might come upon us!" What was the "blessing of Abraham?" We find it in Genesis 12, where God says to Abraham that he is blessed to be a blessing!" The purpose of blessing is to be a source, a conduit, and a distributor of that blessing into a broken, impoverished world. The reason the devil so greatly opposes this teaching is because he does not want the church to be the source of breakthrough and blessing to the nations. He wants to rule them and knows the Scripture: "The rich rules over the poor, and the borrower is servant to the lender!" Slavery has always existed in some form or another. In ancient times, when someone got into debt, they became an indentured slave until that debt was paid off (we see this throughout the Bible). The devil knows that impoverished people are ripe for the picking and will easily give up their freedom for someone to rule over them and give them the basics for survival!

God did not create you to survive but to thrive! The devil wants people looking to the hand of man (human government) rather than to the hand of God. When you flourish independently of men, simply by obeying and trusting God's word and principles, the devil gets mad because you have achieved financial freedom and are no longer dependent upon man. Instead, you flourish under God, bless others, and point them in the same direction – to a God who shows no partiality. God is no respecter of persons, but He is a respecter of principles!

Psalms 35:27 says, "Let them shout for joy and be glad, Who favor my righteous cause; And let them say continually, 'Let the LORD be magnified, Who has pleasure in the prosperity of His servant.'" It's not that God simply "permits" his servants to prosper; the Bible says it gives Him pleasure to see His servants prosper! The devil hates people who serve God and, therefore, HATES the prosperity associated with serving God! Every time you win, every time you flourish and succeed, every time you bless someone – whether by giving over and above, bringing your tithe, buying someone's coffee, or sponsoring a child in a developing nation – you bring joy to your Heavenly Father!

"Not one cent, Not one cent!" That was my father's cry when I announced my desire to resign from engineering and instead attend Bible school! As a proud German, he found a particular pride at his German Club amongst his friends, telling them his son was going to become an engineer. Now, he was mortified, *"How do I tell them my son is becoming a priest?!"* I responded, *"I'm not going to be a priest, Dad! I'm going to marry Leanne..."* It didn't matter. My decision to serve Jesus Christ with the rest of my life was a shame and humiliation upon the family name, a disgrace, and for that, the punishment would be not one cent of financial support in any way! Well, true to his word, he made sure that I "felt" the sting and weight of my choices.

Thirty years later, Psalms 27:10 has become my testimony: *"When my father and my mother forsake me, Then the LORD will take care of me."* God has provided every step of the way. If you had told me when I was in Bible school that I would one day give over one million dollars to the church, I would have told you that you have rocks in your head! Yet, in just 14 years of pastoring this church in San Diego, Leanne and I have given over $1.1 million dollars. Don't measure a life by what you get; measure a life by what you give!

Our church has given away $8 million over the 14 years it has been going, and we started in a hotel ballroom with 67 people, a dream, and a word. We are living examples of God's blessing and prosperity. As Psalm 1:1-3 so poetically puts it, *"Blessed is the man Who walks not in the counsel of the ungodly, Nor stands in the path of sinners, Nor sits in the seat of the scornful; But his delight is in the law of the LORD, And in His law he meditates day and night. He shall be like a tree Planted by the rivers of water, That brings forth its fruit in its season, Whose leaf also shall not wither; And whatever he does shall prosper."* Prosperity is the reward for meditating on God's word and shunning the perishing counsel of the fools in this world! Prosperity is the result of God's favor upon your life! Prosperity is the outcome of God's blessing upon your life! As Proverbs 10:22 says, *"The blessing of the LORD makes one rich and adds no sorrow to it!"*

"And You shall remember the LORD your God," Deuteronomy 8:18 says, "for it is He who gives you POWER to get wealth, that He may establish His covenants in the earth!" Prosperity without purpose is a pathway toward misery. God gives us the power to create wealth so that we can "establish" His covenants in the earth! When we attach Kingdom purpose to our prosperity, it will keep us grounded and rooted. Building the church will safeguard your heart. Seeking first the kingdom of God and His righteousness will keep your soul, marriage, family, and integrity intact. Prosperity without purpose always leads to idolatry and, ultimately, destruction. Wealth was created to establish the kingdom. Genesis 2:10 -12 tells us that "a river went out of Eden and parted and became four river heads. The first is the Pishon, which skirts the whole land of Havilah where there is Gold, and the gold of that land is good!" God gave Adam the great commission to fill the entire earth and exercise dominion. All Adam had to do was follow the river to the first bend, where he would find all the gold necessary to resource the vision and command of God. This is why the devil competes for the gold of the earth; by confiscating it and misappropriating it, he can hinder the establishment of God's kingdom and order.

You were created to flourish. You have been redeemed to prosper. AWAKEN to your destiny to be the head, not the tail, above only and not beneath. AWAKEN to the reality that God desires to use your life to break curses and bring in new levels of blessing everywhere you go. As Genesis 1:28 says,

"Be fruitful and multiply, fill the earth and subdue it, exercise dominion..."

CHAPTER SEVEN

Awaken Divine Devotion

TIME, TALENT, TREASURE

"I will establish one shepherd over them, and he shall feed them— My servant David. He shall feed them and be their shepherd."
Ezekiel 34:23 NKJV

Perhaps my favorite hero in the Bible is David. It's amazing that at the time of Ezekiel, David had been dead for hundreds of years, yet God seemingly pined for, yearned for, and declared that David would be shepherd over Israel. We know that this is fulfilled in Jesus Christ, who, when he walked the earth, espoused all the characteristics and qualities of David. People referred to him as "Son of David." David was far from the perfect man, committing adultery and having an innocent man killed in an attempt to cover his sin, and yet God compares every king after him to David. It wasn't

David's behavior or his righteousness that earned him God's love and approval. It was David's devotion. As a young man, David faced much rejection. A hint into this issue is discovered when Samuel the prophet tells Jesse the Bethlehemite, "One of your sons will be king and sit on the throne over the nation Israel. God has sent me to anoint him." Jesse does something that requires further investigation; he parades his seven sons before Samuel, while the eighth son, David, is sent into the countryside to feed the sheep. At the very least, the father did not believe that there was any possibility that David had the qualifications to be anointed king, but more than likely, it was something much deeper. If one of your sons was to be king, you would bring EVERY child born in your home forward because you would NEVER have to work again or pay taxes. You would enjoy the best of the land!

So why did Jesse send David away instead of bringing him in before Samuel? Why the rejection? A clue might be that when the mother of Eliab and the other brothers are mentioned, it's a different name to the mother of David. Did Jesse feel like there was no way God could anoint a son of a compromising relationship? Was David the son of an affair? Was he the son of a broken relationship? Often, the guilt of our sins condemns us and talks us out of believing for God's best for our lives. Jesse not only thought that there was no way God would BLESS his mistake and indiscretion, but foolishly, he thought he could hide his son from the prophet by sending what was illegitimate into the wilderness and parading his good moments before the prophet of God.

I love God, who declares that His strength is made perfect in our weakness, that His mercy triumphs over judgment, and that where sin abounds, grace abounds even more! (Romans 5:20) after inspecting all seven, Samuel does not find the one God has chosen and asks, *"Is there another?"* Embarrassed and probably blushing, Jesse admits, *"There is still one, the youngest; look he is out there with the sheep!"* Samuel commands him to be brought in, and as soon as young David's body crosses the threshold of the front door, the Spirit of the LORD comes upon Samuel, and God says to him, "RISE and anoint him, for this is the one I have chosen!"

David wrote half of the book of Psalms (75 in total). He wrote the most extravagant poetry. He wrote songs and learned the harp, comforting his soul by singing and pouring out his heart before God. David's worship was his escape, his retreat from rejection, pain, his father's shame, and his brother's mocking. He would sit on hillside after hillside, with no other human around, and he would sing and worship the God of his ancestors. The Spirit of God, drawn by the worship, would fall, and David would feel a sense of calm and peace wash over him. We all have pain, and we all suffer rejection, disappointment, and shame, but we don't all choose God for our medication. Many choose drugs, alcohol, or illicit relationships. Not David – he found his solace in God.

One day, a lion came against this small, feeble flock and stole away one of the lambs. David dropped his harp, picked up his sling, and ran toward the bleeding, scattering sheep. With his adrenaline pumping, he loaded a stone into the sling, ran to gain a proximity advantage where he would be most accurate, slung the rock, and struck the lion. It dropped the lamb, but he knew it would be back, perhaps with more force. Still running toward this dangerous predator, he loaded and struck it again, this time dropping it permanently. He then took a weapon and finished the job, killing it. The sheep were safe. This would serve as a warning to any other predator coming after his sheep.

Well, as life goes, before too long, one day, as David is grazing his sheep in the green and fertile pastures by a forest, a bear comes charging out of the forest and grabs one of the little ones. David immediately drops his harp again, mid-song, and once again "runs toward" this dangerous predator. Loading his sling, he takes aim. This time, the target is much bigger, so David keeps the stone in the sling a few rotations longer to increase velocity and impact.

The stone flies and hits the bear in the head, momentarily stunning the beast, who then drops the lamb and rears up. David, now with weapon drawn, grabs the bear by the beard and strikes to take off its head! Shaking from the adrenaline coursing through his body, he picks up the lamb, which has several puncture wounds, but David knows that with some nursing and care, the lamb will make a full recovery. He doesn't understand why God let this happen. He doesn't know that God was watching, as if...testing. God sees a teenage boy twice risk his life for a few measly sheep. Imagine what he would do as shepherd over my heart, my people, Israel. I believe that it was then that God chose David to be king of Israel. He said he was looking for a man "after his own heart" – a heart that would risk all, sacrifice His own life to save the sheep. God had seen this in private, with nobody watching. He would now set the arena where the entire nation would see the character in his chosen servant. What God witnessed privately would now be on display before the bravest in all of Israel, its army.

Goliath stood nine feet and nine inches tall, heavily armored, heavily defended, and, most awesome of all, UNDEFEATED. He was THE CHAMPION of Gath! He had never known defeat but had crushed and devastated every warrior who stood before him. His size and strength were unmatched. For 40 days and nights, he would present himself morning and evening before

Israel, taunting and mocking them and their God: "Are you not the servants of Saul and I, a Philistine?" In other words, "Didn't God say that when you enter the promised land, I will drive out all your enemies before you? That NO MAN should be able to stand before you? Explain this to me, then. Here I am, unchallenged, undefeated, and unrivaled. Perhaps I am an anomaly? Perhaps when God says, "no man," he meant ordinary men, not descendants of the Nephilim who once terrorized the land in the time of Enoch!"

Israel quaked in their boots. They had never seen a man of this stature and size. He was an enigma, a sight to behold, and they were in awe.

David enters the arena and hears the defiant and mocking insults of this giant. David asks, "Why has no one silenced this beast?" The warriors respond, "Have you seen this man? Surely, he has come to defy Israel!" But David knew the promises of God were more certain and of far greater strength than the might of this hybrid creature. After convincing King Saul that he is able to defeat the Philistine, David puts on his shepherd clothes, takes his sling, goes to the brook, and collects five smooth stones. He wants them to be smooth so they'll fly true, swift, accurate, and deadly. When the giant sees him, he mocks him and then threatens to destroy him. David once again does what he did against the lion and the bear; he runs TOWARD his target, every step gaining him a proximity advantage, closer and closer. Reaching into his bag, he selects a stone and places it into the sling. He begins to wind swiftly, creating speed and torque, and then, like a bullet, lets it go. The giant has not even had time to select from his weaponry a sword, spear, or javelin; it's all happening so fast.

The stone flies like a missile, penetrating the forehead of the giant with such devastation that the giant falls to the ground. David then stands over him, removes the giant's own sword, and proceeds to finish the job, just like he did with the lion and just like he did with the bear. "If you don't kill them, they come again but stronger, in a pack." David beheads the beast and raises the spoil in the air with a shout! The Israelites look on in disbelief and the Philistines in shock; their giant, their hero, is dead – completely annihilated, destroyed. They turn and run in fear. The Israelites now find their courage and pursue the enemy, bringing about a great victory that day and driving the enemy from their territory. God had showcased publicly what He had observed privately! God had His champion, His shepherd, His king, His chosen one.

David was a worshipper. After this great military victory, Saul would summon him to play his music, and the distressing spirit upon Saul would depart. He would find peace and deep, restful sleep. David was a man of honor. Saul put him in charge of one thousand men, and David went in and out before them, earning their respect and honor. Nothing builds honor like giving honor. When you dishonor or withhold honor from others, you diminish honor in your own life. There are three ways we can HONOR the LORD, and there are three tests of DEVOTION. They are **TIME. TALENT. TREASURE.** If you want to be a mighty one in the earth, these are the areas that, when fully devoted to God, shape you into a mighty and blessed servant of God!

1. TIME

Matthew 6:33 says, *"But seek first the kingdom of God and His righteousness, and all these things shall be added to you."* Please note that it doesn't say, "seek ONLY" – it says seek first. When we put God first, He is in His rightful position in our lives. When God is first, He then is released to "add" to you all the things others pursue and strive for. When God is first, He can trust you with money, success, and material things. But when something else takes His rightful place, this is called idolatry, and God restrains His hand from blessing you with more. He will not "add" to that which causes us to stumble and self-harm. I have found that putting God first in my life has been the greatest accelerator of His goodness and blessings in my life. I honestly believe I am blessed beyond anything I deserve. Putting God first is so easy: He has the first say over my life, my time, my decisions, and my money. It means every week, I will rise with my family and attend His house to worship Him. This is called church. I will not miss church because He is first. Each day, Leanne and I begin with coffee and His Word. We give Him the first of our day. Long ago, we decided to see what would happen if we put God first and served in church. I was the "chair-setter-upperer" (my made-up title) for youth each week. I set up the chairs, made sure they were straight, and then prayed that the young people sitting in them would have an encounter with God and be forever changed.

God must have been watching because before long, he gave me people to look after, not just the chairs the people sat in. It was a small group of junior high students on a Friday night. Quickly, the group exploded, and I had the largest small group. Then, I left engineering, following God's call to go to Bible college. From there, we never looked back. Every time you honor God with your time, you will find that God does something magnificent that only he can do with your time and your life. He will make your life one of fulfillment, meaning, and purpose. It's the greatest life. Where are you serving God? Where is He when it comes to your time?

2. TALENT

In Genesis 1, God created man, but in Genesis 2, it says that God formed the man. This means that you do not just exist (being only created); it means that you also have giftings and wirings, the handiwork, and the fingerprints of God's forming in your life. Ephesians 4:8 says, "When He ascended on high, He led captivity captive, and gave gifts to men." God has wired you with certain gifts and talents. Nothing pleases Him more than when we bring these gifts and talents and lay them before Him on the altar, offering them to our Creator to use as He wishes. As you and I offer Him what we have, as little as it seemed to me at first, I had no idea what would take place. I found that God began to bless, increase, and multiply the talents I offered. They say you have to work to make a living, but when you discover your gifts and talents and deploy them, it will feel like you never work another day in your life. I was watching television when I saw the English rock star Robbie Williams say, "I feel like I was born to do this; I was born to sing!" That's a realization that God made me a certain way to do a specific thing. Do you know your wirings? Do you know your giftings? Do you know your talents?

Everything I have brought to God, He has multiplied and increased. A little boy brings five loaves and two fishes to Jesus, and what happens? They multiply and increase, ministering to the multitudes. Bring your gift to God and watch what He does with it. Sadly, you must beware of the devil's enticements when God begins to multiply your talents and gifts. So many who started in the house of God, like Whitney Houston, Jessica Simpson, Brittany Spears, Katy Perry, and many others, had their gifts hijacked and no longer use them to bring glory to God. Instead, they have traded them for their own personal fame and for things that are shiny today and perish tomorrow. You were not created to absorb fame; you were created to reflect God's glory. I decided many years ago that I was surrendering everything to God. It's the most amazing life -- a life of no regrets. Through my penchant for drama, I have been blessed to write two theatrical productions that reach sold-out shows where people are so impacted and moved that they come to Christ. They find more than entertainment – they find salvation. I have written books that have brought miracles and breakthroughs into people's lives. One couple who could not conceive and had negative doctors' reports, who were told their only hope was adoption, found a new faith after reading my book *PUSH (Pray Until Something Happens)*. They conceived and bore a child, and now they have not one but three children.

I always loved to entertain, tell stories, and joke. When I first got saved, I wondered, "How could God possibly use this?" But He breathed upon this gift, and now, each week, I get to use this gift for storytelling to tell the greatest story ever told. There is NOTHING like bringing your gift into the house of God and offering it to be used for the glory of God. It has eternal rewards. You were created by Him and for Him – on purpose and with a purpose.

3. TREASURE

Luke 12:32-34 says, "Do not fear, little flock, for it is your Father's good pleasure to give you the kingdom. Sell what you have and give alms; provide yourselves money bags which do not grow old, a treasure in the heavens that does not fail, where no thief approaches nor moth destroys. For where your treasure is, there your heart will be also."

Did you know that your heart can actually be directed? So many people believe that they can't control their heart. We hear it and see it all the time on the daytime talk shows and soaps: "I can't help it. I just lost my love for my wife, so I left..." or "I knew it was wrong, but I couldn't help it; I fell in love... it's not my fault!" Many people believe their heart governs their life and they are at its mercy. If we lose love for our spouse, then there's nothing we can do to retrieve it again. Many believe that if our heart starts developing feelings for someone else, we are powerless to stop it. The Bible does say in Jeremiah 17:9 that "the heart is deceitful above all things, And desperately wicked; Who can know it?" But the Bible also commands us in Proverbs 4:23 to "guard our heart above all things because out of it flows the issues of life!" How do we do this? I'm glad you asked. Jesus taught us that "where your treasure is, there your heart will be also!" In other words, your heart will follow your treasure. You can lead your heart by where you place your treasure. I bring my tithes into the house of God because I know my heart can easily drift and be seduced by this world's shimmering, shiny, temporary things. But where my treasure is, there my heart will be also! I bring offerings to God because I can easily go "through the motions" in my worship and serving of God. However, I want to keep the passion alive, so I bring offerings over and above the tithe, and bam! I am passionate about God, His kingdom, and His priorities!

God made your heart to follow your treasure. Too many people allow their treasure to follow their heart and lose their souls in the process. As you devote your treasure to God, you will also begin to see him increase the flow of this treasure in your life. The word TITHE means "tenth" or test. God never TESTS you to fail you; instead, he ALWAYS tests to promote you. Can you devote to Him your treasure – or at least just the first tenth? When we do, we will find that we live with his blessing and multiplication on the other ninety percent. Our testimony is this: the greatest thing we have ever done was devote our TIME, TALENT, and TREASURE to the kingdom of God! When you make God the focus of your treasure, He will make His treasure focused toward you!

Jesus said in Luke 6:37-38, "Judge not, and you shall not be judged. Condemn not, and you shall not be condemned. Forgive, and you will be forgiven. Give, and it will be given to you: good measure, pressed down, shaken together, and running over will be put into your bosom. For with the same measure that you use, it will be measured back to you." Notice here that Jesus is saying that you and I determine the quality of our lives by controlling the issues and treasures of our heart. If we judge others, we ourselves come under judgment. If we condemn others, we come under condemnation, but when we forgive others, we receive the freedom that forgiveness brings. When we give, it will be given to us, pressed down and shaken together and running over. The measure we use is measured back to us.

In other words, Jesus says that we set the amount of return! As 2 Corinthians 9:6 says, *"If we sow sparingly, we reap sparingly, but if we sow bountifully, we also reap bountifully!"* Devote to God your TIME, TALENT, and TREASURE and watch what God does in and through and with your life! Get ready – you are about to enter into the greatest season of your life! It's time to AWAKEN the blessing of almighty God on these three areas in your life.

As you begin to awaken to a new vision and a new expression of God's love for you, you will sense a new surge of power. You will see God break off demonic strongholds, and you will find freedom from destructive paths, patterns, paradigms, and powers. You will view the current culture clash with new insights and new revelations. You will begin to experience new hope in your family as God obliterates generational curses and restores generational blessings that will resonate through your family line for decades, even centuries, to come. And you will awaken to a new mission, a new flow, a new level of devotion from and for the King of Kings. Just as I experienced the world through transformed eyes when I was born again, you, too, will find yourself awakening to new levels of peace, joy, hope, and restoration in Him. The best is yet to come. Awaken!

Get To Know Pastor

Jurgen & Leanne

Jurgen and Leanne met in Wollongong, Australia where they attended the same church and youth ministry. Jurgen was employed at BHP Steel as an apprentice studying Mechanical Engineering, when he felt the call of God to leave and attend full-time Bible college at Power Ministry School (now known as Hillsong College). They started dating at the end of his first year in Bible College. After graduating, Jurgen moved to New Zealand as part of a Hillsong church plant. After six months of running the youth ministry at South City Christian Life Centre, Jurgen travelled back to Australia to marry his sweetheart Leanne! After their wedding and some tearful goodbyes to family and friends, Jurgen and Leanne traveled back to NZ to resume pastoring the youth at South City Christian Life Centre.

During the seven years they were in New Zealand, Jurgen and Leanne had a profound and long lasting impact on the city of Auckland especially amongst its youth. Jurgen had become a popular speaker in colleges and high schools and had grown and developed the youth ministry at South City CLC to make it one of the largest in the nation at that time. They had also welcomed their first two "kiwi" sons Jordan and Ashley. In the summer of 1998 Jurgen and Leanne felt a strong call from God to move back to Australia. They sold their home and packed up their boys and belongings and planted themselves in one of Australia's most incredible churches, C3 Church, Oxford Falls..

Under the amazing leadership of Pastors Phil & Chris Pringle they were appointed as youth pastors. In the fall of 2001 they welcomed Tommy, their third son and presumably their third and final child! In the seven years they were part of the team at C3 Oxford Falls Jurgen and Leanne grew the youth ministry to over 750 strong and pioneered the hugely successful Phenomena youth conference that hosted over 3000 delegates from Australia, New Zealand, and around the world. In the fall of 2004, Pastor Phil approached Jurgen and Leanne about starting a church in San Diego, California. Having never even been to San Diego, they both were hesitant about moving, but it didn't take long before God confirmed the move. In the summer of 2005, Jurgen and Leanne and their three boys packed up all their belongings and moved to San Diego. On August 20th, 2005, Awaken Church had its first service and an attendance of 50 people. In 2008, after many years of wanting a girl to add to the family, Jurgen and Leanne welcomed beautiful baby Zoe into the Matthesius clan.

Pastor Jurgen and Leanne invite you to join them at any of the Awaken Church locations which now reach into San Diego, CA, Salt Lake City, UT, Boise, ID, and Seattle, WA. For more information check out, awakenchurch.com.

Made in the USA
Middletown, DE
20 February 2025

71539233R00056